WOMEN ON DEATH ROW 2

Following the success of the first volume of
WOMEN ON DEATH ROW, top crime writer
Mike James presents this compelling new collection
of true stories about women waiting to walk the last
mile as they endure the interminable anguish of
living in the shadow of the executioner.

Will the phone ring at the last minute bringing a
reprieve? How will they spend their last few hours
in the death cell? Will there be hysterics, or heroism?

Their stories are stark and chilling, but they make
compulsive reading...

WOMEN ON DEATH ROW 2

Mike James

truecrimelibrary

Published by True Crime Library,
the paperback division of Magazine Design
and Publishing Ltd.
PO Box 735, London SE26 5NQ, UK

An imprint of True Crime Library

Cover design by Ben James
Designed and typeset by Declan Meehan
Printed and bound in Great Britain by
CPI Cox & Wyman, Reading, Berkshire

ISBN 978-1-874358-41-1

For J

PREFACE

Women killers. To some it's an oxymoron that defies all reason. But the grim fact is that women do kill, and at least in some American states they continue to be executed.

If Death Row is a sad and lonely place for condemned prisoners, this book will show what a hell on earth it is for condemned women. What makes it particularly horrific is the wearisome appeals procedure. The system is designed to be democratic and foolproof, and perhaps it is, but the long wait, the endless appeals, the stays of execution and the rejected pleas have a devastating effect on the mindset of a condemned woman. How many Death Row inmates, one wonders, when they finally enter the execution chamber, are any longer in a sound state of mind?

The debate over capital punishment is set to run and run. Half the American people still want it. They point to the murder rate in the US being one of the highest in the civilised world, and they point to capital punishment as their protection. The other half, who don't want it, point to the fact that almost anyone can get a gun in the US, and a gun is a murder weapon. They also point to the grisly ritual of this Old Testament revenge system as something that doesn't belong in the third millennium.

How would you feel if you knew you were to be executed tomorrow? What must it be like to walk the last mile?

Suddenly you come face to face with apparatus that will shortly snuff out your life. Will you be brave, conduct the last minutes of your life without fuss, or will you slump into a state of hysteria? You would be a most unusual person if you did not feel anxiety and fear, even if you cloaked it successfully.

The majority of the women executed in America during the 20th century walked the last mile with great courage, but for some it proved a terrible ordeal.

Eva Coo was one of the brave ones. When she was

dispatched in Sing Sing's electric chair in 1935, she waved to prison wardresses and gave them a cheery, "Goodbye, darlings."

And when Juanita Spinelli was escorted into the San Quentin death chamber she arrived early. Witnesses had still to take their seats. Asked if she wanted to return to her cell while they filed in, she said without emotion, "No, we'll just stand here." The door of the lethal chamber was open and the bags of cyanide were clearly visible.

"Does this offend you?" she was asked. She replied, "Oh, no, the sun's out, isn't it? It's a beautiful day." And as the visitors took their places the condemned woman continued to chat about the weather. Finally, when everyone was ready, she walked calmly into the gas chamber and sat in one of the chairs. "It's time, keep your chin up," she told the warden.

When cop-killers Irene Schroeder and Walter Glenn Dague were on Pennsylvania's Death Row, Ms. Schroeder was dubbed "Iron Irene" because of her fortitude.

"Don't worry about me, I'll be all right. You'd better go back to Glenn. I think he needs you more than me," she told the chaplain as she approached the death chamber. Walter Glenn Dague was still in his death cell – he wasn't due to follow Irene to the chair until days later.

When she had taken her place in the electric chair she was asked if anything could be done for her. She replied: "Yes, there is something. Please tell them in the kitchen to fry Glenn's eggs on both sides. He likes them done like that." Her story is in Part Three of this book.

Not everyone was so brave as Irene Schroeder. One horrific execution at Sing Sing in 1936 saw a woman being carried to her death. Mrs. Mary Frances Creighton had been having a love affair with Everett Applegate. Since Applegate was already married, both of them considered that his wife, Ada, was in the way, and decided to kill her.

Although Applegate contended that he had nothing

to do with the actual killing, it was proved conclusively that he had conspired with Mary to commit the murder, and he was executed at Sing Sing immediately following her electrocution.

Applegate met his fate bravely. But several days prior to the date set for the execution Mary began to show signs of cracking. Whenever the door of the death house opened and a prison official came in, she would study his face intently as he approached.

A moan of disappointment would emerge from her lips if the official said a word or two to a guard and then left, for the only idea in her mind now was that she might be reprieved.

On the day before the execution the warden entered the death house and went directly to her cell. She could see at once that he had news for her. Like a trapped rat, she watched his approach, her eyes dilated, mouth open, the blue veins in her neck showing how her heart was pounding. She shrieked when the warden shook his head. "I'm sorry," he said, "but the state governor has refused to intervene."

Mrs. Creighton burst into a paroxysm of weeping and, after exhaustion had apparently overcome her, lay as if in a coma for several hours. The officers became fearful that there might be a shocking scene when she reached the execution chamber.

There was a shocking scene, but it did not take place in the execution chamber. It occurred about a half-hour before, when the unhappy woman suddenly became hysterical, shrieked and raved and then collapsed. She was not unconscious, but was completely paralysed by fear, so much so that the officers were unable to get her to the execution chamber either under her own power or by holding her up on either side.

Finally they decided to place her on a hospital trolley and wheel her through the death house door to the electric chair, the first time this had been done at Sing Sing. When she was lifted off the trolley she had to be held down in the chair until the straps were placed around her, otherwise her limp body would have sagged to the floor.

Perhaps the way she died was merciful – after all, she was probably unaware of it.

The roles were reversed when so called lonely-hearts killers Martha Beck and Raymond Fernandez went to the electric chair at Sing Sing in March, 1951. Fernandez was stricken with fear and had to be supported, his legs giving way under him.

Martha followed him, relaxed and seemingly unconcerned after consuming two whole chicken dinners.

Probably the most infamous American Death Row double-act was Ruth Snyder and Judd Gray, who were found guilty of the murder of Ruth's husband. Their story is also included in this book.

Even executioner Robert Elliott admitted that when he drove to Sing Sing to electrocute the couple on that night in January, 1927, it was one of the few occasions when he felt his nerve shaken. He had tried not to read the newspapers, but the headlines screamed that the woman he was about to kill was already in a death-like stupor. Her hair had turned white, her eyes were sunken, she chattered madly, and she wept and prayed continuously.

They tested the chair. It was in perfect order. Then the witnesses were escorted into the room, to occupy four rows of benches brought in from the chapel. At last the prison clock struck 11.

If you had been outside the door that leads from "murderers' row," the last abode of the condemned, you would have heard Ruth's heart-rending moans and Gray's anguished cries for her. One minute later the ghost of what was once the brazen Ruth Snyder was brought from her cell. Two matrons walked beside her, holding her lightly by the arms. Tears streamed down her cheeks. She was white. She trembled convulsively.

You can read how she died in Part Three of this book. It was a horrific business. But that's what the judicial killing of women is – a horrific business.

CONTENTS

PART ONE

1 – HER HUSBAND WAS BURNED ALIVE
Marilyn Plantz

Many people who knew them thought that Jim Plantz, 33, and his wife Marilyn, 27, had a perfect marriage. The sort of marriage that caused people to say, "Whatever else happens, nothing will ever destroy that couple until hell freezes over."

That was certainly the story that Marilyn, a pretty, slim woman with an abundance of long, black hair and a slightly nervous smile, put around the neighbourhood.

"They're a marvellous couple. They don't have any problems," said one of Jim's sisters. "They never fuss, they never argue."

Their next-door neighbour, Ken Taylor, also figured they were "pretty happy people." Jim Plantz, he said warmly, was a good father, who spent every available hour of his spare time with his children, nine-year-old Trina and Christopher, six.

The Plantz family moved into their quiet residential neighbourhood in Midwest City, Oklahoma, in December, 1987, and Ken Taylor, offering the hand of welcome, liked them at once. "Jim was a really fun-loving guy. He built a playhouse for his kids," he recalled. "He was a whiz with wood and electronics."

Mr. Taylor often spoke over the fence to Jim Plantz. He spoke less often to Marilyn because he found her less forthcoming, but he liked her. "If they were having any family problems, you couldn't tell it," he said.

But who can really tell anything about the closed doors of a marriage? What looks good on the domestic surface is seldom the subject of much further inquiry. Most neighbours take what they see as being what there is. But Ken Taylor's son Tim didn't think like that. He knew instinctively that the Plantz marriage was a sham. He had no doubts, he was to say, that Mr. and Mrs. Plantz "fought all the time."

Tim had got it right. A marriage rarely works when the parties are both young teenagers, living in the romantic expectation that nothing will change in their lives over the next 50 or 60 years. Married at 16, Marilyn blossomed out to become a woman of moderate beauty and increasing frustrations. After 11 years of matrimony she was fed to the teeth with her home-making, utterly reliable husband. Since they moved into their new home, their marriage had deteriorated into turbulence. All behind closed doors, of course, with only a few cracks that young Tim Taylor managed to peer into.

Jim Plantz was particularly distressed by the increasing rows. He told Marilyn, "If you leave me I'll commit suicide. I can't live without you."

Jim worked at night – he was assistant press supervisor at the *Daily Oklahoman*, the state newspaper whose big rotary presses ran noisily through the night, spilling out thousands of copies to land on morning breakfast tables. Usually he would get home at about 4.45 in the morning, have a snack, and then peel off to go to bed, where he would stay until after midday.

On Sundays he was a Sunday school teacher, a role that was in line with what everyone said of him: he was a punctual, dependable employee, a devoted father, and a good, honest American Christian.

One thing neighbour Ken Taylor did notice was that soon after Jim went to work, around seven o'clock in the evening, Marilyn would put her two children in the car and drive off. "I don't know where she went, but it was usually pretty late when she got back."

Even so, his suspicions were not aroused. He was flabbergasted, therefore, when, much later, he learned that Marilyn, whose marriage he thought was so perfect, had a teenage lover, was a prostitute and a drug addict, and habitually spent her evenings in the company of thieves and low-lifers.

According to the police, on those evenings when Ken Taylor saw her leaving the house after her husband had gone to work, she would take the children to a baby-sitter, then drive to a park, where she sold herself for sex to get money for drugs.

Her teenage lover was William Bryson, who was just 18. One night after a vigorous sex session Marilyn confided to him: "I want Jim out of the way. Kill him for me and we'll go away to Texas and get married."

Bryson, who made no living except as a petty crook, was reasonably fond of his married lover, who was half as old as him again, but he wasn't quite prepared for that sort of heavyweight proposition. It wasn't so much the prospect of killing that bothered him as the fact that he had hardly a cent in the world. How could he keep her after the first bloom of romance wore off? He had never supported anyone in his life apart from himself, and he made a bad enough fist of that. He stiffened and drew away from her.

But Marilyn was persuasive. She knew all the feminine arts, and she was certain she could get him on her side. They were both into sex and drugs and regularly got high together. She was well aware that Bryson was dysfunctional, unpredictable, and the sort of teenager that her husband's friends would dismiss as a weirdo.

Sensing his initial concern, she teased his ear and spoke in a soft, honeyed tone. "I've got two life policies on him. If he dies the payout stacks up to more than three hundred thousand bucks. That's plenty enough and more for us to live on."

Slowly Bryson started to relax. Now she was beginning to make sense. He loved the sound of money. Already he was beginning to put together some possible scenarios.

"I'll need an accomplice," he said. "I think I know who'll help us. He's a friend of mine, a guy called Popeye."

Popeye's real name was Roderick Farris, who was on remand for stealing a car. Bryson met up with him the next day.

"I've been hired to do a killing," he said jauntily, like a man announcing he had just got a contract to clean a supermarket. "I can arrange for you to have ten grand for yourself if we can make it look like I had no part in it."

3

"Who's the guy you want bumped off?"

Bryson looked around warily, just to be sure no one was in earshot.

"My girl friend's old man." He lowered his voice. "She came by my apartment an hour ago and she was crying her eyes out. She said her husband had just beaten her up for no reason at all. She wants me to do him in."

Later that day he took Farris to meet Marilyn in a supermarket car park. "This is Popeye, the one I told you about, who's willing to kill your old man for ten grand," Bryson said. Marilyn replied: "It'll have to look like an accident." They sat in Marilyn's car, discussing a variety of ideas. Then Marilyn said: "You could drown him on a fishing trip. That would be a good idea because he can't swim."

Farris, who was silent throughout most of the discussion, was becoming increasingly dismayed. Finally he said, "I don't want no part of it." Next day he was jailed for stealing the car. He did not help in the killing.

Undeterred, Bryson called in another friend, one who turned out to be much more malleable. Clinton McKimble, 18, cocked an ear when his friend told him what he wanted. But there was no way he would do it for a mere ten grand.

Bryson took him to see Marilyn at her home while Jim Plantz was at work, and they did a deal. McKimble was to get $45,000 for shooting Jim Plantz as he drove home from work. Marilyn went to her husband's gun cabinet and took out a double-barrelled shotgun.

"This one will do," she said.

August had arrived, a hot, sweaty month in Oklahoma. That August night in 1988 storms were rattling away in the background and rain pelted down in squally, intermittent showers as Bryson, at the wheel of his car, and with McKimble alongside him with the shotgun across his knees, sat in the darkness outside the printing works of the *Daily Oklahoman*. It was 3.30 a.m.

Patiently they waited for Jim Plantz to emerge at the

end of his shift. They knew that it was always around a quarter to four, and that he always drove home in his pick-up truck.

The rain was coming down so fast when he came out that they only just recognised him. Bryson hurriedly put the car into gear and headed after their prey.

"Quick, pull level with him," McKimble said urgently. Bryson gunned the engine and the car swerved out as if to pass the pick-up. Just then a truck came speeding down the road from the opposite direction. Irritated, the driver flashed his lights, forcing Bryson to pull back. By the time the road was clear again, Jim Plantz's pick-up had vanished into the wet, misty darkness.

"We've lost him," Bryson said helplessly. "Damn that truck driver!"

Marilyn, who knew the killing was set for that night and was lying awake in bed, was stunned when her husband walked through the door. When later that day she learned what had happened she bit her lip, aware that the tension was getting to her. But she cheered up when Bryson folded his arms around her and kissed her passionately.

"Honey," he said, "I'm not giving up. I love you too much. We're going to try again as soon as possible. Gimme a beer and we'll work out a new plan."

In the early hours of Friday morning, August 26th, 1988, three weeks after the botched attempt outside the *Daily Oklahoman* printing works, Marilyn let Bryson and McKimble into her home. She gave them some beer and all three of them snorted cocaine. Then they fell asleep.

They awoke with a start at around 3.45 a.m. Marilyn gave them her son's baseball bats, and showed them where to hide. When they were settled she went up to her bedroom.

At 4.25 a.m., crouching in the darkness of the suburban home, the two men heard Jim Plantz's pick-up arrive on his driveway. A minute passed, then, as he came through the front door and walked into his living-room, whistling and toting a bag of groceries, they leapt

5

on him, crashing the baseball bats down on his head and his body.

Staggering, raising his arms to protect himself from the rain of blows, Plantz yelled out, "Marilyn!" But Marilyn wouldn't come. She lay awake in bed, oblivious to his petrified screams, while her two hired assassins beat Plantz into unconsciousness.

When they had finished she came down into the living-room and stared down at her husband's crumpled body. Jim Plantz was still alive, and was moaning softly, in a half-conscious state. "Look at him," she said, her voice betraying exasperation. "It don't look like no accident right there. Take him away somewhere. You're going to have to burn him. Make it seem like a traffic accident. Be quick, the kids will wake up in a few minutes."

As she fetched a bucket of water and a cloth and began to wipe up the blood from the living-room carpet, she was unrecognisable from the suburban housewife who all the neighbours regarded as the perfect all-American woman.

Bryson threw the body on to Plantz's own pick-up and drove out to N.E. 50th Street, a secluded, woodland area in eastern Oklahoma County, followed by McKimble, who was driving Marilyn's car. They put the body behind the steering wheel of the pick-up, splashed a can of petrol over it, and some of it over Plantz himself, and threw a match on to it.

Incredibly, Jim Plantz wasn't dead. Still just conscious, he became aware of the flames all around him, aware that he himself was on fire. The two killers, peering through the smoke and flames, watched in horror as they saw him slowly pull himself up in the middle of the inferno.

His arms began to thresh, his legs swung outwards in an agonising, desperate attempt to escape from the blazing truck. He was too late. The flames enveloped him and he slumped back to be burned alive.

An hour or so later, as the sun rose on another soggy day in Oklahoma, a fire engine alerted by an early-morning motorist pulled in alongside the still burning wreck. As soon as the firemen had extinguished the remains of the fire, the dead, carbonised body slumped across the front seats was revealed.

What was clear to them as they radioed for help was that the victim had tried desperately to get out of the blazing truck. He had opened a door and got his left leg out before being overcome by the flames and smoke. Whoever he was, they surmised, he had died a terrible, agonising death.

The corpse was burnt beyond all recognition, but the police quickly identified the vehicle and that led them to Marilyn Plantz. She played the part of the grief-stricken wife like a movie star. Comforted by a policewoman, she wept on the phone, clutched her two anxious children to her skirts, broke the news to relatives between sobs, and everyone believed her.

"Poor Marilyn," they said softly to each other. "What a hell of a terrible thing for her to go through."

Jim Plantz had died in his own blazing truck in the early hours of Friday morning, which left the police all that weekend to put together their various options. The post-mortem revealed that he had first been beaten, and that he was undoubtedly alive when the truck was set on fire. Who, they needed to find out now, would want to kill this amiable, decent family man, print worker during the week and Sunday school teacher at weekends?

They asked a few questions and it wasn't long before they fond out that the death of Jim Plantz would enrich his wife through his insurance cover by a hefty six-figure sum. So they began to figure that perhaps Marilyn had hired someone to kill her husband. And then, pretty sure they were on the right track, on Monday morning they arrested her and charged her with murder. It didn't take long before she broke, coming up tearfully with the names of her accomplices. Next day they arrested Bill Bryson and Clinton McKimble.

While he was in a police cell waiting to be charged Bryson, overcome by fear or remorse or both, tried to hang himself with his shoelaces. He was taken to hospital and afterwards returned to the cell. There he tried to drown himself in the toilet, but that was another botched attempt.

He told the police: "I didn't have no specific reason why I killed him. All I was thinking while I was beating him was all the times she came up to me with a black eye and crying. I didn't like that."

Marilyn said, "I had nothing to do with Jim's death. He never came home that night. Everyone knows we had a perfect marriage, and we also had a great sex life."

But he did come home that night. When police searched the Plantz home they found Jim's bloody work keys in Marilyn's underwear drawer, effectively establishing he was right there in the house when he was beaten. That she tried to hide the keys in her underwear drawer was more evidence that Marilyn was nowhere near bright enough to plan a perfect murder.

When the trio were first brought to court two months later, it was announced that the prosecution had agreed to let Clinton McKimble plead guilty to murder and be sentenced to life imprisonment. As part of that agreement he would testify against Marilyn and her lover.

The full trial, with Clinton McKimble as the prosecution's chief witness, opened in March, 1989. Marilyn wept as he described the way they ambushed Jim Plantz in the living-room

"Bryson came out at him and hit him in the arm and the head with his bat. He yelled 'Marilyn!' and fell to the ground. I ran out and started hitting him too. We hit him about ten times with the bats. Marilyn was in the bedroom. She said she didn't want to see her husband when we did that to him."

But she did come to the front door to give them her car keys when they put her still-moaning husband in his pick-up.

"Bryson drove the truck out to a nice quiet place, with me following in her car. First I set fire to a rag in the truck's gas tank to try and blow it up, but the rag went out. So Bryson doused Plantz and the truck with a liquid and lit him up."

When they returned to the house to drop off her car, Marilyn was still cleaning blood from the living-room carpet with a brush, soapy water and a rag. She gave them some of her husband's clothes so that they could change out of their bloodstained clothes. Later they tossed their bloody clothes in a river.

As McKimble described the killing to a hushed court, Marilyn doodled on a pad of paper and chewed her fingernails. When she was shown the photo of her husband's burned body, which was presented to the jury as an exhibit, her eyes widened.

Neither she nor Bryson gave evidence on their own behalf. Bryson's defence lawyers described Bryson as "delusional and too mentally incompetent to testify." They also made much of the fact that they didn't like the way the trial was being handled. They thought the two defendants should have been tried separately, and they criticised the judge for refusing to allow the jury to see a videotape of Bryson's confession to the police. The reason was that the tape was too damaging to Marilyn's case, which would not have been an issue if there had been separate trials.

In the videotape the teenage hit man swung his arms back and forth as he demonstrated how he ambushed Jim Plantz. "We was hitting him everywhere...just swinging," he said.

Another witness, a 17-year-old, said that Bryson and McKimble told him how they had killed Jim Plantz, and they were laughing about it.

Roderick Farris, the man Bryson first tried to hire as an accomplice, told the court that the day he had refused to help he was at the Plantz home with Bryson and McKimble because they were all planning to steal a truck, and they were killing time until it got late. They later stole the truck and Farris was arrested for theft at about 3 a.m. The other two were not arrested.

While he was waiting in the house that night, he said, Marilyn and Bryson were hugging and kissing. Then a neighbour arrived. As the neighbour walked in Bryson picked up a kitchen knife and McKimble picked up a hammer and both said, "If this is her husband we're going to take him out."

The jury took less than three hours to find Marilyn and Bryson guilty of killing Jim Plantz, of conspiracy to murder, of recruiting others to help, and of arson. They deliberated for another five hours before voting for the death sentence in both cases.

Before the various appeals and stays of execution that were to drag on for another dozen or so years, there was an obligatory clemency board hearing on June 6th, three months after the jury's verdict. At this hearing Bryson chose to speak for himself, telling the board that in any case "persuading the majority of this board to vote to spare my life is impossible." Three of the four board members, he reasoned, were appointed by the state governor, which made him their employer.

"The governor has made his position crystal clear regarding capital cases. Therefore your job security demands that you respect the governor's wishes. The vote of the governor and the vote of those he has appointed will forever be one and the same."

He was right in his surmise. The board voted 4-0 against clemency.

After the ritual of failed appeals, Bryson sat down to his last meal in the death cell, a couple of hours before midnight on June 16th, 2000, when he was due to die by lethal injection. He had a plate of 10 fried shrimps, with salad, a strawberry drink, a slice of German chocolate cake, a pint of ice cream and a hot apple fritter.

Thirteen relatives and friends of Jim Plantz were gathered in the death chamber audience. As Bryson lay on the execution table he said he bore no ill will to anyone. Several times he said how sorry he was, and smiled at members of his family in the audience. He said, "I love you Dad. I love you, Sharon. I love you, Auntie." He referred too, to Marilyn's children, Trina and Chris. "I'd like to tell them how sorry I am. Get over the pain and get on with your life."

Bryson left behind a child of his own, a 12-year-old

boy who is being bought up by Bryson's father.

Marilyn Plantz, his cold-blooded associate, had to wait for nearly another year to pass before all the appeal options were finally exhausted. During her 13 years on Death Row she had become a born-again Christian and had become reconciled with her daughter Trina, who was nine when her father died.

"I can't bear the thought of knowing she is going to die," Trina said. "I feel like she deserves a second chance. I don't want my mother to die."

Relatives reported that there was no reconciliation though with her son Chris, who was six when his father died. He visited his mother in jail and wrote to the parole board about the pain the murder had caused him. "Can you even try to imagine, in your worst nightmares, having your father killed in the very next room with the bat he taught you to hit with the day before?" he asked.

Two hours before she was due to die Marilyn had her last meal. The order was meticulously recorded on the several sheets of official paper detailing her last hours. It consisted of a chicken taco salad, a Mexican pizza, two encharitos, some cinnamon twist, a slice of pecan pie and two cans of Coca-Cola.

Six hours before the scheduled 9 p.m. execution in Oklahoma's State Penitentiary on May 1st, 2001, she had been moved to a special cell only eight paces from the death chamber.

At five minutes to nine, Judge Niles Jackson, who had been invited to join the audience of relatives, friends, reporters and a clutch of Oklahoma state officials, walked down through the prison hall. A door bordered in yellow paint interrupted the stark white walls. It led to the execution "viewing rooms." Already the other inmates on Death Row had begun what has become an execution ritual – a cacophony of sound as they kicked and banged their cell doors.

Judge Jackson and other members of the audience sat down in a viewing room that had two rows of chairs – 24 altogether. They all faced a large glass screen, but a white blind temporarily blocked out their view. The death chamber was on the other side of that window. Behind the judge's room was another room, with one row of chairs and another large glass screen.

As the audience settled down they could see human silhouettes moving behind the white blind. They heard muffled noises coming through a speaker in their room. On one occasion they saw an arm go up, as if to open the blind. Judge Jackson, who wrote about the experience afterwards, felt his pulse begin to race, especially when nothing happened.

Finally the blind was raised, like the curtain in a theatre, and for the first time the audience saw Marilyn Plantz. "She was just six feet in front of me," the judge remembered afterwards. "The clearness hit me suddenly. It brought clearly home that this was going to happen. I was actually going to watch a woman die. She lay stretched out on a table, covered with a sheet up to her chest. Her arms were resting on table extensions out to her side. The sheet hid the leather and fabric fasteners that bound her to the table."

Twelve members of the Plantz family were also in the audience at her execution. Many of them wanted her dead – they had campaigned for her to die for nearly 13 years.

A doctor inserted one intravenous needle with a tube attached into each arm. The tubes would alternate, carrying the three poisons of the lethal injection. The eyes of the audience followed the tubes as they disappeared into an adjoining room.

In the execution chamber with Marilyn were two prison warders, two deputy warders, one doctor and a chaplain. One deputy warder stood next to the black wall telephone that had a direct line to the governor's office in Oklahoma City. It never rang.

The director of the Oklahoma state corrections department, who was sitting next to Judge Jackson, broke the silence. "Let the execution begin," he said.

The warder standing next to Marilyn asked her if she

had any last words. She did, and quoted a passage from the Bible.

"I have overcome the world," she said quietly. "Nothing, absolutely nothing, can separate us from the love of God. If you all want to see me again, you must be born again." She also thanked her family members for being there, turning her head slightly to look at each one and saying their name. She made no mention of the crime for which she was about to die.

She finished speaking, turned her head straight and closed her eyes. She seemed to be calm and at peace. The warden nodded towards a window into which the tubes ran and said again, "Let the execution begin."

The chaplain began reading from his Bible. There was no sound or movement as the three poisons were fed through the intravenous tube into Marilyn's arms and body.

The first chemical injected was 50 cc of sodium thiopental. This was to render her unconscious. The line was then flushed with saline. The second chemical was pancuronium bromide – again 50 cc. This was to stop her breathing. Again the saline flush. The third and last chemical was potassium chloride, another 50 cc. As this poison enters the body the heart stops.

Each chemical was injected into the intravenous line by a hand-held syringe, each syringe held by one of three people who were chosen after extensive interviews.

Marilyn's chest stopped moving within five seconds. She lay still, motionless. Judge Jackson remembered looking at the clear tubes to try to detect the poisons entering her system, but he could see nothing. He could, however, hear slight noises from the heart monitor the doctor had earlier attached to her chest. He also heard slight noises from her mouth "almost like snoring." Then nothing.

The audience waited. The visiting rooms were soundless except for an occasional stifled sob from a relative. No one moved. Some looked away, and then back again. Judge Jackson began to feel clammy and felt his heart beat faster. Once again he reminded himself that he was watching a woman die.

After three minutes Marilyn's skin turned an almost purple colour. The doctor approached, lifted her eyelids, placed a stethoscope on her chest and listened. He glanced at a wall clock and in a bland voice void of all emotion said, "Death occurred at 9.11."

The blinds were lowered and the audience was escorted out to a waiting van that would take them to their parked cars. Their minds still filled with the horrific vision of the last 15 minutes, no one spoke. A cold wind, carrying squalls of rain, swept the prison yard. It was a night just like that one nearly 13 years ago when Jim Plantz died.

The last 11 minutes of Marilyn Plantz's life in which she was publicly executed revealed her as a woman of exceptional courage. Those few minutes left the invited audience numb with shock, left some of them speculating if the state had got it right, whether such an agonising scene could be equated with justice.

They must have wondered, did she really deserve this dreadful, ritualistic legal killing in the prime of her life? Could such savage yet clinical retribution really expiate even the most awful crime? Could anything that a woman had done merit such a cold-blooded execution?

Opponents of capital punishment frequently quote hangman Albert Pierrepoint's famous aphorism: "Capital punishment serves no purpose but revenge," as if it were profound and philosophical. But Pierrepoint's reputation stands on his ability to tie knots – he was neither an expert nor a philosopher on the ethics of capital punishment. For as anyone could have told him, all punishment in the Western world is revenge, since we do not seek to rehabilitate or reform criminals.

What should we think of someone like Marilyn Plantz, misguided to the point where she became a killer for her callous and brutal selfishness? Should she be pitied as a woman lying helplessly on the execution table, with lethal poisons being fed into her veins, or should we remember dependable Jim Plantz, betrayed and horrifically beaten and burned alive at her icy command?

At least most of Jim's family can come up with an answer to that.

2 – A GRUDGE AGAINST THE WHOLE WORLD
Lynda Lyon Block

Lynda Lyon Block had a massive grudge against society. Anyone in a uniform, any official, any edict or law, any suggestion that she should toe the line for the benefit of other people, made her go ballistic.

You meet people who rail against the rules during the journey through life, but you wouldn't meet many who took things as far as Lynda. She was obtuse, difficult, feisty – a perpetually angry middle-aged woman.

It wasn't always quite as bad as that. Lynda came from a privileged, well-heeled background. The daughter of prosperous estate agents, she did well at college and became a freelance journalist and a respected member of her community, holding various appointments with local civic organisations in Orlando, Florida.

But she seemed determined to be an oddball, marrying a man who was 37 years older than herself, and writing articles that seemed to be in defiance of everything that the rest of us take for granted.

What might have been just a rebellious streak turned to something far weirder when in 1991 she went to a meeting of America's anti-government Libertarian Party.

America has for long been the home of far-out parties with obscure and impossible aims. In the mid-19th century there was even a party called the Know-Nothings, which exploited the rising resentment of native Americans against Irish and German immigration.

Originating from a secret society, its members, when challenged, were supposed to say, "I know nothing." They had surprising but brief success for a year, and then faded – they reeked too much of prejudice for respectable Americans to stomach.

So the Libertarian Party, which was against any form of rules and regulations, not only provided an ideal platform for Lynda's nihilistic views, but also enabled her to share them with like-minded people.

During a break in the party meeting she found such a like-minded person – a kindred spirit who dovetailed into her conception of national government. He was George Sibley, and despite the fact that there 15 year's difference in their ages – she was 43, he was 58 – his views did not dominate her. They were simply two people who recognised each other for what they were.

Like Lynda, Sibley came from a privileged background. Like Lynda he was a fierce defender of civil liberties, resisting every restriction on what he believed to be his rights. Like Lynda, he was destined to become a killer.

Theirs was a chance meeting, and an instant meeting of the minds. At the time Sibley was refusing to pay a new tax on local services. Lynda eagerly supported him in his crusade. She told him excitedly how she wanted to switch to anti-government journalism.

"I want to publish a regular anti-government newsletter," she told him as they talked over a cup of coffee. "But I need about $20,000 to get started, and there's no way my family will put up that sort of money."

"I will, though," Sibley replied. He was already finding Lynda's band of enthusiasm infectious. The bond was forged.

Later it was forged physically. Unmindful of her aged husband, the 79-year-old father of her young son Gordon, Lynda leapt into bed with Sibley. When her husband found out, he moved sorrowfully out of his house in Orlando and Sibley moved in with Lynda. A few months later, however, the ageing Mr. Block launched court proceedings to recover his home.

Lynda now regarded Sibley as her common-law husband. There would be no wedding – they didn't want anything like a marriage licence, which they regarded as bureaucratic interference.

Meanwhile, the anti-everything newsletter had got off the ground and was becoming something of a success. It concentrated on tips on how to avoid paying income tax, which gave it widespread appeal to many Americans. The problem for the publishing couple was that if

Lynda's husband got a court order instructing them to leave the house, they would have nowhere to continue publishing.

How could they persuade him to leave them alone? The answer they hit on was nothing if not novel. They broke into the flat where he was living, tied him to a chair, gagged him with duct tape, and demanded that he abandon his efforts to get his home back.

To show that they meant business, Lynda stabbed him in the chest with a small knife. Sibley closed the wound with duct tape and they left him, in great pain from his wound, still bound to the chair, and unable to summon help.

The neighbours were the first to realise that something was wrong. Unable to get any response from their persistent knocking at Mr. Block's front door, they called the police. Officers broke in and found the old man just as Lynda and Sibley had left him. Although weak from his ordeal, he was able to describe what had happened.

Lynda and Sibley were arrested and charged with aggravated battery committed against a person over 65, and jailed to await trial. When Lynda's husband refused to press charges, the state prosecutor was determined to go ahead. The case dragged on for another two years, until July, 1993, when Lynda and Sibley agreed to plead no contest in return for probation. They were then released.

Later they claimed: "We were pressurised into all this. We were threatened with long terms of imprisonment if we didn't co-operate. Accordingly, we withdraw our plea."

They hadn't yet appeared in court for the probation sentence, so the state's attorneys were effectively back where they started. And the two accused were about to make things really difficult for them.

"We are sovereign citizens of the United States and as such all federal and most state laws do not apply to us," they declared.

To make this claim they were using the Thirteenth Amendment – not the constitution's Thirteenth

Amendment which prohibits slavery, but a Thirteenth Amendment they claimed was ratified in the 19th century and then swept under the carpet in a government plot against citizens' liberty.

This was not a new dodge. Others wanting to protract their sentencing had used it in the courts. The amendment originally stated that any citizen of the United States ceased to be one if he accepted titles of nobility from an emperor, king, prince or foreign power. It was floated at a time when the country was jealously guarding its republic status, and the Supreme Court's answer to it was always the same – that it was only a proposed amendment that had never been ratified by Congress.

Lynda and Sibley rejected that answer. In support of their case they invoked the judge who was scheduled to hear their courtroom plea. "His name is preceded by the word 'Honourable,' which is a title of nobility making him an alien with no authority over us," they declared.

American lawyers, accustomed to weird-o defence pleas, scratched their heads. All of them were aware that the prefix "Honourable" before the name of an American judge is merely a courtesy honorific and of course confers no nobility on its holder.

Lynda and Sibley weren't done yet. They declared that marriage licences, driving licences and social security numbers were illegal, and when asked by police her date of birth Lynda replied: "I discovered just the other day that I never had a date of birth."

When the day arrived for their court hearing, they sent a fax to the judge, the county sheriff and local newspapers. It declared: "We have barricaded ourselves in our home and we will resist any attempts to take us by force. We will not live as slaves, but would rather die as free Americans."

They had a bit of a shock, though, when instead of a horde of sheriff's deputies laying siege to the house, a lone deputy drove up to the garden gate, knocked on the door, and, receiving no response, shrugged his shoulders and departed.

Alone and concerned about the outcome, especially for Lynda's son, nine-year-old Gordon, the couple wondered what would happen next. Almost certainly, they reckoned, armed police would come to lay siege to the house. There were other less likely possibilities, but they could hardly take on the entire might of the Florida state police force.

"Let's get out of here while we can," Sibley said.

They loaded their Ford Mustang with their favourite possessions, including guns and more than 1,500 rounds of ammunition. Then they headed west, quite certain that somehow they were going to elude a system they didn't believe in by simply driving into another state.

As he was bundled into the car, little Gordon was terrified. He didn't like Sibley and he was old enough to realise that his mother was taking on something she couldn't handle.

When a bail bondsman called a few days later he found the house empty. A hunt began for the fugitive couple but nothing more was seen or heard of them for several weeks. Then, at about lunchtime on October 4th, 1993, they surfaced in the small town of Opelika, Alabama, where they stopped to buy provisions at a Wal-Mart store, and for Lynda to phone a friend in Orlando.

Sibley and Gordon waited in the Mustang in the car park while she made her call from a kiosk at the front of the store. Sitting in the driver's seat, Sibley didn't notice what Gordon was doing. But a horrified passer-by did. She saw the little boy mouthing the words "Help me" to her through the back window.

She looked around desperately, and then spotted a police patrol car parked nearby. Anxiously she waited for the policeman, Sergeant Motley, to exit from the store, where he was buying office supplies for his department.

Motley listened to her story, nodded curtly, and drove round the car park to assess the situation. He pulled up behind the Mustang, got out of his patrol car, walked over to Sibley and asked to see his driving licence.

"I don't have those sort of damned contracts with the state!" Sibley shouted. He got out of his car and began to rant against the government, claiming that it had no authority to tell him what to do.

"Step away from your car, sir," the sergeant ordered.

"No, I won't," Sibley replied.

The sergeant placed his hand on his holstered gun. His intention probably was to scare this awkward customer, but he was too late. Sibley drew his own gun and began shooting.

Motley ran to his patrol car, probably to radio for back-up, but Sibley went after him, still firing. In the phone box, Lynda heard the shots, dropped the receiver, pulled out her 9 mm pistol, and ran towards the wounded sergeant.

As she came up to him she emptied an entire 14-round clip of bullets into his body and his car, finally shooting him in the chest as he turned to face her.

Mortally wounded as he was, Motley unhooked his radio-telephone and called for help. Sibley and Lynda jumped into the Mustang and drove eastwards on back roads. Sibley had difficulty holding the wheel – he had been hit in the arm during the gunfight. Motley's fate was far worse. When an ambulance arrived he was rushed to hospital but died shortly after admission.

Incredibly, the whole tragic incident stemmed from the fact that the bizarre couple were too pig-headed to accept a sentence of probation for tying up and wounding a man nearly 80 years old.

The police set up roadblocks that the fleeing Mustang couldn't ultimately dodge. The car was stopped, but Lynda and Sibley refused to get out or to give up little Gordon. In the four-hour standoff that followed the afternoon drifted into evening. With a cordon of cops surrounding the Mustang, the occupants called out to them to ask for a TV set. They also asked, more bizarrely, if they could meet the Pope.

When finally they realised that further resistance was futile, they surrendered. The little boy was put in the care of foster-parents, while Lynda and Sibley were driven off to police headquarters, to be charged with capital murder.

Anti-government activists immediately rallied to their defence, protesting that the two killers had only been trying to stop law-enforcement subverting a citizen's right to roam the country freely.

Lynda's defence for her atrocious crime was equally pathetic. In a statement she said she and her partner had gone on the run to avoid imminent arrest. They had to do this, she claimed, because a friend who was supposed to prepare the paperwork they needed to stop action on the judge's order had let them down.

Sibley said: "When I saw Sergeant Motley's hand move towards his gun, I instinctively reached for mine, and that made the situation irreversible. I knew that once he reached cover behind his car he would certainly fire at me, so I fired at him."

And Lynda added angrily: "There has to be a point where you decide you're not going to take injustice any more. The fact that he had a badge and a gun makes no difference to me. I reacted instinctively. I defended my husband."

The plea of self-defence went right on into the courtroom. But witnesses were clear that it was Sibley who fired first, and just as clear that Lynda joined in the shootout after Sergeant Motley was wounded. Forensic experts argued over who actually fired the fatal shots and couldn't decide on the answer. But it didn't much matter anyway, because Lynda and Sibley were both convicted of capital murder and sentenced to death.

As is the time-honoured method in America, Sibley launched himself into the appeals process. But Lynda, now 54, would have nothing to do with the appeals to which she was legally entitled. True to all her convoluted beliefs, she claimed that the courts were corrupt, and she rejected the help of lawyers.

She contended that Alabama had never regained its status as a state after the American Civil War, and therefore its courts had no jurisdiction over her. "If they don't want to give me justice, that's life," she said philosophically. "At least I'll have died fighting. I want the blood on their hands."

That perhaps in summary was what it was all about for Lynda Block – she wanted to die fighting, and fighting anyone. She wanted blood on someone else's hands, just for the hell of seeing it there.

The question has to be asked in all the circumstances, was Lynda Block mad, and did she team up with a madman? This was a question that no one asked, because everyone involved was quite sure that this was merely a headstrong woman who was unable to control herself. As a result, she killed an innocent man and threw her own life away.

The wonder remains, of course, that anyone can work themselves up to the point of expressing so much hostility to authority that they are prepared to sacrifice their life for it. Even if it is difficult to comprehend, it is undoubtedly senseless.

Her execution was set for April 19th, 2002 – the anniversary of the Waco fire and the Oklahoma City bombing. Then it was postponed, without any given reason, until May 10th.

Sergeant Motley's widow, Juanita Motley, commented: "I believe the delay is intended to avoid putting her to death on a date significant to other people who share her anti-government views. I don't want to make a martyr out of her. If that's the reason, I prefer it to be May 10th."

But Juanita Motley also said she wanted the Alabama Department of Corrections to lift its ban on Lynda talking to reporters. "If they don't let her speak to the press or whoever, her supporters will figure it's just another government cover-up. That way the authorities are playing into her hands."

In the event, Friday May 10th, 2002, it was. On that day Lynda Block went to Alabama's 75-year-old electric chair at Holman Prison in Atmore, to become its 176th victim and the first woman to be executed in the state for 45 years.

She may also turn out to be the chair's last occupant. Under a new law, after July 1st, 2002, the state's condemned prisoners were to be put to death by lethal injection unless they specifically opted for electrocution. Nebraska was left as the only American state still using the electric chair as its primary method of execution.

Asked if she had a last statement to make before she was electrocuted, Lynda replied, "No."

A prison spokesman commented: "She seemed to be somewhat stoical. She displayed no emotion."

Was that perhaps because at the last moment she was reflecting on the wasted, completely futile life she had lived, combating anything and everything that other civilised people took for granted? For Lynda Block couldn't even be dignified with the title of revolutionary. She was just a public nuisance.

3 – PICKAXE DOUBLE-MURDER
"GAVE ME AN ORGASM"
Karla Faye Tucker

Karla the Killer gave a whoop of triumph as she plunged her pickaxe into her two victims. "Each time I hit them with it I had an orgasm," she declared.

A drug addict at nine – "my mother and I were real close; we used to share drugs like lipstick;" a prostitute at 12, a double killer at 23; the first woman to be executed in Texas since the Civil War at 38 – Karla's short sojourn on Earth left a bloody page in the annals of American crime.

The horrific events of the worst night of her troubled life began in the early hours of June 13th, 1983. With her boy friend Daniel Garrett and a man named Albert Sheehan, she went to the Houston flat of another man she knew, one Jerry Dean, 27.

The intention of Garrett and Sheehan that night was to collect some cash and some motorbike parts. Karla went along with them because she had something else in mind. She was bearing a bitter grudge against Jerry Dean for destroying photographs of her late mother, and she would later say that she wanted to "whip his ass."

When the trio arrived at the apartment Dean had company. He was asleep in bed with 32-year-old Debra Thornton, a girl Garrett had met at a party.

That night all hell broke loose in the apartment. The slaughtered bodies of Jerry Dean and his woman friend Debra were found by one of Dean's friends shortly before 7.30 next morning. The friend had called to see why Dean had not turned up to give him a lift to work, as they had arranged. He phoned the police, who arrived to find the corpses sprawled on a blood-soaked bed. The three-foot handle of a pickaxe protruded from Debra Thornton's chest.

Blood spattered the walls and ceiling. Jerry Dean's wallet and car, and Debra Thornton's handbag, were missing, together with some motorbike parts.

Dean lay on his back completely naked, his upper torso displaying horrendous wounds. Debra Thornton, the handle of the pickaxe in her chest pointing to the ceiling, wore only a blood-soaked T-shirt.

A pathologist reported that each victim had been struck 21 times. Jerry Dean had also been beaten on the head with a heavy instrument that had smashed his skull.

His missing car was found abandoned three days later. Like the pickaxe, it bore no fingerprints.

Detectives assigned to the case got nowhere. None of the street people and informants usually aware of what was going on at night seemed to know anything. Then, a few weeks later, Detective Sergeant J. C. Mosier was looking through a file on another case when his eye fell on a familiar name.

That name was Daniel Garrett who, it seemed, had been among the associates of Jerry Dean who had already been interviewed by detectives but dismissed from the case for want of evidence.

Mosier had been on familiar terms with Daniel Garrett in the past, but had lately lost touch with him. He still occasionally chatted to Garrett's ex-wife, however, and reasoned that this might give him an "in" on the case where his colleagues were only achieving stalemate. He phoned Garrett's former wife and arranged to see her.

"Are you still friendly with Daniel's family?" he asked when they met. She was, she said. In that case, could she help him?

"I want to find out if he really was involved in the Jerry Dean murder case," he said. "Talk to them. Find out anything you can. If he was involved, they must know something."

The woman went off, deep in thought. A few days later she phoned Mosier. "I talked to my ex-brother-in-law," she said. "He thinks Danny was somehow involved in the double-murder." She paused, and then spoke slowly. "My ex-brother-in-law is frightened. He wants to talk to someone, but he doesn't want to get involved."

"Tell him to call me," said Mosier.

When the detective's phone rang some minutes later the nervous relative identified himself. He agreed to meet Mosier on condition that the detective was alone. To Mosier's surprise, however, when he turned up for the agreed rendezvous the relative was accompanied by a woman.

"She's related to Danny Garrett's girl friend, Karla Tucker," the informant said somewhat mysteriously.

Mosier persuaded them that it was their duty to go with him to see the district attorney, who in turn got the man to agree to being fitted with a concealed microphone and tape recorder before initiating a conversation with Danny Garrett and Karla Tucker at Garrett's apartment.

Outside in the street police officers with radio equipment were ready to eavesdrop on the conversation.

They heard Garrett's relative tell the pair that they had become prime suspects in the double-murder investigation. To this Karla replied scornfully: "They're just digging."

The relative asked if the victims were asleep when they were killed.

"Jerry Dean woke up," Garrett told him. "The girl Debra started waking up. I told her to stick her head under the covers."

"Hell," Karla said. "I had an orgasm with every swing of that pickaxe."

Daniel Garrett was arrested on July 20th, 1983, as he left his home to go to work. Karla Tucker, still inside the apartment, was also arrested. A third person then broke cover, running from the flat. Caught and arrested two blocks away, he said his name was Albert Sheehan.

Garrett and Karla wouldn't talk, but Sheehan was more co-operative. He said he had accompanied the other two to Jerry Dean's apartment on the night of the murders, but he left when he realised what his companions were going to do.

The detectives believed him, and with Sheehan agreeing to testify as a prosecution witnesses against the two accused, the rest was plain sailing. Garrett and

Karla were each charged with both murders, Sheehan with burglary.

Karla Faye Tucker's trial for the murder of Jerry Dean and Debra Thornton began on Wednesday, April 11th, 1984. Albert Sheehan, the prosecution's star witness, told the court that he and the two accused had spent the day drinking, taking drugs and smoking pot before they set out for Jerry Dean's apartment.

"When we arrived Garrett and Karla went into the flat while I looked around outside for Dean's car. When, shortly afterwards, I went to the apartment, I heard a gurgling noise coming from the bedroom. I went to investigate. The sound was coming from Jerry Dean. Karla was attacking him with a pickaxe.

"She was standing over a body on the floor. The body was covered in a sheet and she was striking the pickaxe into the sheet and the body. She was pulling on the axe, wriggling it and jerking it. She finally got it out and held it over her head. She turned and looked at me, smiled, and did it again."

"Next night, as we watched a television newscast about the killings, Karla was ecstatic. She was very proud of what she had done. She thought that what they had done was something spectacular."

The relative who initially blew the whistle on the two killers told the court how they had come to his home at 5 a.m. on June 13th, telling him they had stolen Jerry Dean's car and some motorbike parts which they wanted to hide somewhere. They said they had "offed" Dean two hours earlier.

The relative explained why Karla hated Jerry Dean. He said that Dean had destroyed Karla's photos of her mother in revenge for her teaming up with his wife and cleaning out his bank account. Dean wanted to break Karla's friendship with his wife.

Karla's defence counsel called no witnesses. Asking the jury to convict her, he said he would seek a life sentence in a bid to save her from the death penalty. The jury duly found her guilty after retiring for 70 minutes.

Next came the trial's penalty phase. A woman

psychiatrist, who interviewed Karla for five hours, said that the defendant told her she was into marijuana at the age of nine, heroin at 10, and had been on hard drugs ever since, except for a two-week period. At the time of the double-murder she hadn't slept for three days – she had been taking narcotics, drinking and injecting speed every two to three hours.

The psychiatrist doubted that Karla got a sexual kick out of the killings. In fact, Karla told her she hadn't had a single enjoyable sexual experience in her whole life.

Speaking at last for herself, Karla told the jury: "I don't see how anybody could ever be forgiven for something like I've done." If someone treated her the way she had treated the victims, she said, that would not be justice enough.

The background of the attack on Dean sprang from the day when he took a photo album of hers and stabbed and cut up the only photographs of her mother. "I just never could forgive him," she said.

She had used a key taken from Jerry Dean's wife's home to enter the apartment that night. "I followed Danny into the bedroom. The light was out. There was a little crack in the curtains with some light coming through. I could see the silhouette of a body sitting up. At that point I knew it was Jerry. I went to him, sat down on top of him, and told him to shut up.

"He said, 'Karla, we can work it out. I didn't file charges.' He was referring to the fact that his wife and I had used his bankcard to clean out his account. He grabbed my arms. We started wrestling. Danny came up and got between us. I saw the silhouette of Danny beating Jerry on the head with what seemed to be a hammer."

She turned on the light, she said, and saw that Danny had broken off the attack. "Then I heard a noise, a gurgling sound. It was coming from Jerry. Danny walked out of the room and I was left standing there. I kept hearing this sound. All I wanted to do was to stop it. I saw a pickaxe leaning up against the wall. I reached over and grabbed it. I swung it and hit him in the back with it."

But after she had delivered four or five blows, Jerry Dean was still gurgling. "When Danny came back in, I told him to make Jerry stop that noise. Danny took the pickaxe and swung it several more times, hitting him in the back. Then he turned him over and hit him in the chest, and the noise stopped."

She said that Danny then left the room again and she realised that there was someone else in the bed, lying beneath the covers and shaking.

"My mind, I don't know where it was at. I picked up the pickaxe again. I swung it, but it didn't penetrate. I tried it again a second time, and when I did the person came up from under the covers. It was a female, and she grabbed the pickaxe."

At this point, she said, Danny came back into the bedroom again and she left. When she came back he was striking the girl with the pickaxe. "The girl was sitting, and the pickaxe was real deep in her left shoulder. She had her hands on the pickaxe. She said, 'Oh, God, it hurts! If you're going to kill me, please hurry up!' He hit her again, and put the pickaxe right there in her chest."

Despite the evidence on the undercover tape, she denied she got a sexual thrill with every swing of the pickaxe. She only said this to impress Danny. To her, the killings were unreal. "I do not remember seeing any holes or any blood." Nor did she smile at Sheehan, she said, as she swung the pickaxe.

The jury retired but they were back with their verdict in less than three hours. Karla Tucker, they decided, must be sentenced to death.

Daniel Garrett's trial followed in November, 1984. Brought from Death Row to testify, Karla told the court that she loved him very much. The reason she was giving evidence against him was slightly convoluted. "I testified once for me. I had to do that to more or less set myself free," she explained. "Now I'm doing it because people deserve to know the truth."

She told the court that Danny Garrett had been training her to become a hit-woman, and she took part in the attacks during the double-murder because "it seemed the right thing to do." She went on: "Danny said he was going to make me one of the best hit-women around. He said he could more or less train me. He could get the jobs, I could make the hits, and we could make lots of money.

"He talked of killing a lot of people, sort of assassin work. It fascinated me. I wanted to know what it was like and what he felt."

The five-foot-three budding hit-woman described how Garrett took her on army-style exercises in which they crawled, camouflaged, along ditches, aiming guns at imaginary enemies. She said that after the double-murder her boy friend "bragged on me, like I'd passed some sort of test. He told me that he was proud of me that I didn't turn and run."

She was asked about a conversation she had had with a woman friend. She admitted that she had told this friend that she had done the murders by herself.

Convicted of murder, Daniel Garrett was sentenced to death on November 29th, 1984. But he never made it to the execution chamber. He died of a liver complaint in 1995 while still appealing against his death sentence.

Meanwhile, Karla Tucker had become a born-again Christian. In 1996 she married Dana Brown, her prison padre, from whom she was to remain separated by a glass screen whenever they saw each other. They were not even permitted to touch during their last tearful meeting only hours before her execution.

"The other Karla no longer exists," she told viewers in a TV interview. "I'm so far removed from the person I used to be out there."

And this seemed to be true. Opponents of her execution included one of the jurors who convicted her, plus a brother of Debra Thornton and a sister of Jerry Dean. Even hard-boiled Detective Sergeant Mosier was convinced of her conversion and thought she should be spared.

"I'm an old cop and we don't go for that 'I'm reborn in prison' stuff," he said. "But I believe it with Karla."

In another prison interview she recalled how as a child she envied another little girl whose parents took her to church. She longed to go to church too. The other child's parents "saw right where I was headed. If they had just reached out in the love of Jesus and tried to help me, you never know how they could have changed the course of my life…I'm telling anybody who's out there, there are things you can do to save a child from going down that road."

As the execution date approached all too quickly, how did she fancy her chances of a reprieve? Some days, she said, she could see the Lord working that miracle. On other days, "I can see him coming down and escorting me home from that table. So I try to feel like, 'Okay, Lord. Whatever. It's up to you.'"

For Karla and her supporters, however, the outlook didn't look good, even when the influential TV evangelist Pat Roberson lent his weight to her cause. "I am not opposed to the death penalty," he said. "But in this case I think her sentence should be commuted. She's paid the price. God forgave her, and so do I."

Karla's fate was in the hands of the governor of Texas, one George W. Bush, soon to become the US president. Throughout his governorship of Texas, a state renowned for its busy death chamber, he had never so much as delayed an execution, let alone commuted a death sentence to imprisonment for life. His practice was to ask if there were any question of a condemned prisoner's guilt. He also asked if the appeal courts had examined all the material. When the answers to these questions were "Yes," as they always were, and as they were in the case of Karla Faye Tucker, the execution went ahead as scheduled. In 1997 Texas had carried out half of all the executions that took place in the whole of the United States.

The only factor that might have saved Karla was Texas's reluctance to execute women. Before her, the last woman to be executed in the state was Chipita Rodriguez, put to death in 1863 for killing a horse dealer.

"I think it all comes down to an attitude," said Victor Streib, an influential US lawyer. "Texans just don't treat their women that way." His view was echoed by Mike Charlton, a distinguished Houston attorney. If Karla were executed, he said, it would be hard for most Texans to deal with, except for the most rabid death penalty supporters.

But after visiting her in jail, Victor Rodriguez, chairman of the state's Pardons and Paroles Board, said he remained convinced that an offender's gender should not be a consideration in matters of clemency. And what Rodriguez said counted – Governor Bush could not commute a death sentence to life imprisonment even if he wanted to if the board didn't recommend a reprieve.

Assistant District Attorney Roe Wilson expressed the hardliners' attitude: "The fact that Karla Tucker is a woman is irrelevant. What is relevant is that she committed the offence, admitted to it and bragged about it afterwards."

Before her execution, informed opinion had it that she would die, ironically becoming the victim of her gender, the one thing that many believed might have saved her. Because a reprieve for Karla, it was argued, would invite charges of sexism and claims that there wasn't equal justice for all.

So she kept her date with the lethal needle as scheduled, on Tuesday, February 3rd, 1998, shuffling shackled, a nappy in place beneath her prison dress, to the death chamber at Huntsville Prison.

4 – SHOULD SHE HAVE DIED?
Wanda Jean Allen

In the middle of the 19th century an American construction worker named Phineas Gage was preparing dynamite to blast a hole in the ground when the powder exploded prematurely. The iron rod Gage was using was blown through his head and his brain and exited through the top of his skull. By some trick of fate he survived.

That is to say, his head and his body survived. But something strange happened to his mind. He had a complete change of character. From being an urbane, affable young man, he became an offensive, obnoxious fellow, unable to keep a job, drifting from one place to another without purpose.

This is a classic symptom of what happens when the prefrontal-limbic area of the brain is damaged in a young person – the part that controls emotions, judgment and general behaviour. In other words, an injury such as Phineas Gage sustained, or even just a violent bang on the head, can change a model citizen into an anti-social one, or perhaps even into a psychopath.

The condition is now recognised and beloved of lawyers who are having difficulty defending a prisoner on a capital charge. Anything that the defendant can come up with that resembles a bang on the head in childhood is seized upon, for conceivably that means his personality was changed and he therefore can't really be held to be responsible for his actions.

While this defence is sometimes cynically exploited, medical evidence does show that a violent head injury can change a docile person into an unpredictable one. When he was 18, the serial sexual killer Fred West fell off a fire escape, struck his head on a concrete floor and was unconscious for 24 hours. His family claimed that he was never aggressive before that happened and that it was only afterwards that he was subject to tempestuous rages and mood swings.

Let us now consider Wanda Jean Allen. At 12 she was hit by a truck and knocked unconscious. At 15 she was stabbed in the left temple, in the prefrontal-limbic area of her brain.

After the incident involving the truck Wanda was examined by a psychologist who calculated her IQ at 69. The psychologist recommended a neurological assessment because she showed symptoms of brain damage.

Wanda's life was a complete mess for as long as she could remember. Her problems climaxed in 1981 when, aged 21, she was sent to jail for shooting dead her childhood friend Dedra Petrus. In prison she met Gloria Leathers, who became her lesbian lover. She served only two years, and when she was released Gloria went to live with her at her home in Oklahoma City.

It was a turbulent relationship. There was one row after another, and on more than one occasion each called the police to their home.

Another row flared up on the afternoon of December 1st, 1988, while they were at a local grocery shop. The dispute continued when they returned home, and ended dramatically outside a police station.

During the row Gloria told Wanda that she had decided to move out because she was fed up with their constant feuds. Wanda, who was still serving the suspended part of her sentence for manslaughter, started a fight and Gloria set out for the police station to complain.

Wanda was later to claim that Gloria struck her in the face with a rake while they were indoors. She ran out of the house to fetch the police and Gloria, still clutching the rake, chased after her. Outside the police station Gloria came at her again with the rake, whereupon Wanda shot her through the chest.

"It was simply self-defence," she claimed. Marks left by the rake were still visible on her face when she was photographed in jail. Four days later Gloria died, and Wanda was facing a murder rap.

Her family approached a local lawyer, Bob Carpenter, to defend her. Believing it was a non-capital case, he agreed to represent her for a fee of $5,000, and Wanda's family made an initial payment of $800. Then Wanda was charged with first-degree murder, the state announcing that it would seek the death penalty. Carpenter was somewhat taken aback – he had never handled a capital murder case.

When he learned that Wanda's family could not pay the $4,200 he would need to hire an investigator and expert witnesses, he asked the judge to allow him to withdraw from the case, offering, at the same time, to act as co-counsel for free if the court pointed a public defender as lead counsel.

But the prosecution would have none of it. For a number of legal reasons they objected to Carpenter's request and the judge upheld their objection, refusing to allow Carpenter to withdraw. He had no alternative now but to defend Wanda single-handed, with no previous experience of capital cases, no investigator, and no money to engage expert witnesses.

Wanda was brought to trial in 1989, where the prosecution portrayed her as a dominant lesbian who intimidated her lover. Defending her sexual orientation, she protested: "It didn't make either of us less human than if we were in a heterosexual or bisexual relationship. We are still human. We have emotions. We laugh. We cry. It was part of our life."

There wasn't much hope for Wanda in that courtroom. Predictably, she was sentenced to death. But when the appeals procedure began, Bob Carpenter filed an affidavit. In it he stated that it was not until after the trial that he learned that Wanda was mentally impaired. He cited the notes of the psychologist who examined her when she was 15, and who said she showed symptoms of brain damage, none of which he knew about. "I did not search for any medical or psychological records, or seek expert assistance," he said.

Another psychologist was brought in to examine Wanda. He found "clear and convincing evidence of cognitive and sensory-motor deficits and brain dysfunction," possibly stemming from head injuries received during her adolescence. He also found that her intellectual ability was markedly impaired, and assessed her IQ at 80. He cited "particularly significant hemisphere dysfunction" impairing Wanda's "comprehension, her ability to express herself logically, and her ability to analyse cause-and-effect relationships."

He concluded that she was consequently more liable than others to become disorganised by everyday stresses, and thus more liable to lose control under pressure.

On Death Row Wanda, a self-proclaimed Baptist, and Marilyn Plantz, who was to be executed four months later, shared the same shower cubicle. They were allowed three showers a week, each limited to 15 minutes. They had to eat their meals alone, on trays deposited through door slats.

When the weather was good they were shackled and led to a narrow, high-fenced area. Their hand and leg chains were removed, and they were free to exercise for one hour.

Their contact with the outside world was limited to television, letters and voices through clear plastic dividers and telephones. Only a few relatives and visiting clergy were allowed to look at them. No one except prison officials was allowed to touch them.

Commenting on the two executions, Oklahoma's attorney-general, Drew Edmondson, said: "Gender is simply not relevant to the legal process. But of course whenever you have someone of a different gender or background they tend to attract more attention."

A woman hadn't been executed before in the state in modern times, he added, because none of their cases had progressed that far: "It simply hasn't been their turn yet," he said.

In 1999 the UN Commission on Human Rights called on nations not to impose the death penalty on a person suffering from any form of mental disorder. This cut little ice in Oklahoma, where the governor's mansion was occupied by Frank Keating, a death penalty supporter.

Refusing Wanda's request for a 30-day stay of execution, he said, "This is not easy because I'm dealing with a fellow-human being, a fellow-Oklahoman."

Outside the Oklahoma City jail where Wanda had spent 11 years on Death Row, the Rev. Jesse Jackson was among two dozen death penalty opponents arrested for blocking the roadway. "She must not die in the dark. She must not die alone," he said. "We intend to be with her all the way."

Wanda, now 41, was then taken 130 miles to the Oklahoma State Penitentiary at McAlester for her execution by lethal injection on Friday, January 12th, 2001.

As the deadly chemicals were about to be administered, she said, "Father, forgive them, for they know not what they do." Just before she closed her eyes a member of the defence team signalled "I love you" from behind the glass separating witnesses from the death chamber. She raised her head and smiled and a tear could be seen in the corner of her eye.

Something else told her she was not alone. The other prisoners could be heard beating on bars and shouting their support for her. She was pronounced dead six minutes after she received the injection. She had become the first black woman to be executed in America for nearly 50 years, and the first woman put to death in Oklahoma since Dora Wright was hanged on July 17th, 1903.

"Any state that exercises this ultimate punishment against a person who is mentally impaired is acting not only immorally but also irrationally and illegally," said Ajamu Baraka, acting director of Amnesty International USA's programme to abolish the death penalty.

"I think it's Oklahoma's embarrassment," said Ellen Wisdom, another protester. "I think it's appalling, the number of people we're willing to execute in this state."

Oklahoma is second only to Texas in its number of executions – Wanda Jean Allen was the second of eight prisoners the state planned to put to death in a period of four weeks. Her death brought the total executed since the US Supreme Court lifted its ban on executions in 1976 to 686.

5 – "DON'T LET HER KILL ME!"
Lois Nadean Smith

For very different reasons, Greg Smith and his mother, Mrs. Lois Nadean Smith, had a big grudge against Cindy Lee Baillie. She would have to die, they decided – and die very slowly.

Greg Smith didn't like Cindy, who was a former girl friend of his, because he believed she was trying to get a hit-man to kill him. Why Cindy, who was only 20, should want to do this no one knew.

Lois Nadean Smith – always Nadean to her few friends and countless enemies – wanted her killed because she believed Cindy was a police informer and had told police about her and Greg's involvement in drug dealing. Other acquaintances of the Smiths were to say, however, that Nadean wanted to kill her because Cindy was supposed to be pregnant by Greg.

Whatever their reasons, there can be no doubting their method. They decided to bring in Dolores Finn, Greg's current girl friend, to help them. It was scarcely dawn on July 4th, 1982, when Nadean phoned Dolores and asked her: "How would you like to go boogie?"

The expression meant "go to a party," and if 5 a.m. seems a little early for a party, it should be remembered that July 4th is Independence Day in America, a public holiday when everyone has lots of fun with their friends and family.

Dolores at first didn't understand what Nadean meant. She asked to speak to Greg. "What's your mom on about?" she asked him.

Greg explained that his mom had been drinking, but their plan was to pick up Cindy Baillie in their Cadillac and they would all go to an Independence Day party.

That didn't seem a brilliant idea to Dolores. Cindy Baillie was her rival for the hand of Greg Smith, and wasn't therefore an ideal companion for a holiday. She knew that Cindy was staying in a motel in Tahlequah, Oklahoma, which was 50 miles distant, a long way to take a trip before the sun had hardly risen. Still, Dolores figured she would enjoy the ride anyway.

But on the way to Tahlequah Dolores began to have serious misgivings. She didn't like some of the things the Smiths, sitting in the front seat of the car, were saying about Cindy Baillie. She began to wonder if there was going to be some trouble ahead. If that was going to happen, she didn't want any part of it.

When they reached the motel, Nadean Smith, a short, stocky and powerfully built woman, banged on the door of Cindy's room. "Do you want to come to a party with us?" she yelled.

Cindy came to the door. "A party?" she asked. "Where is it?"

"At Gans," Nadean replied. Gans was 50 miles away, but still in Oklahoma state.

It didn't take Cindy a second to make up her mind. She was a party animal, and this was Independence Day. But as she went to get into the car Dolores put out a restraining hand. "I don't think you should come," she whispered. "They may be up to no good."

Cindy laughed. "I can take care of myself," she replied. She got into the back seat of the Cadillac alongside Nadean. Greg drove, with Dolores beside him.

Given the warning she had just received, and given what she already knew about Nadean Smith, Cindy was taking a terrible risk. Nadean had a fearsome reputation for being a bully. She was a hard-looking woman with short, reddish hair and a tough way of speaking. Her son Greg was taller and slimmer, and Cindy was well aware that he too was a tough-talker.

They hadn't gone very far towards Gans when Nadean started to pick a row. "You snitched on Greg," she told Cindy. "You've been trying to set us up, haven't you?"

"I don't know what you're talking about," Cindy protested indignantly. Slowly Nadean took a pair of black gloves from her handbag. Her face was contorted with hate and venom. She drew on the gloves, then, with a sudden fluid movement, seized Cindy by the throat in a tight pincer grip. "You're never going to see

Tahlequah again, my lovely!" she snarled.

Before Cindy could cry out, Greg took a paring knife from Cindy's handbag and held it aloft. "Look at this, mom," he said. "She was going to hurt you with it."

Nadean grabbed the knife. "Were you going to hurt me with this, bitch?" she demanded. Again, there was no time for Cindy to reply before Nadean thrust the blade deep into her throat, twisted it, and pulled it out slowly.

Cindy screamed. Tears of fright and pain sprang from her startled eyes, the tears mingling with the blood streaming down her dress.

While she wept uncontrollably, clutching her injured throat and trying to stem the flowing blood, Greg drove on, just as if nothing had happened. An hour later, the car pulled up at a suburban house. This was the home of Paul and Sadie Dolan. Paul was Nadean's ex-husband.

When the events of that day were subsequently reconstructed it was never quite clear why Nadean Smith had chosen this particular place for the "party" she evidently had in mind.

The Smiths arrived with the injured Cindy at about 7.30 a.m. She appeared terrified. She was bleeding from the neck and blood was soaking into the bodice of her dress. Nadean Smith ordered her to go to the bathroom and take a shower.

On her way to the bathroom Cindy passed Paul Dolan. She paused to plead with him to help her.

According to Sadie Dolan, who was to tell at least the first part of the story of what happened in the Dolan house, Nadean then said: "You can say anything you like to me, my ex-husband and his wife. It won't do you any good. It's gone too far."

After Cindy's shower, Sadie continued, the occupants of the house all sat together in the living-room and, in front of the intended victim, began discussing killing her.

"Cindy was begging for us to help," Sadie Dolan went on. "Nadean said they had to kill her, or Greg would be killed." Sadie had no idea why that should be so, or what they meant by that. She went on: "Nadean asked my husband to take them to the Sixty Acres to kill Cindy. Paul replied that they could not get there because the creek was up. Besides, he didn't want to get involved.

"I heard Nadean say, 'The girl is going to have to die slowly,'" Sadie went on. "Then Cindy said she wanted to die fast. She was going to have a baby and she was concerned about the baby."

Sadie, evidently thinking there was trouble ahead, left shortly after that to go to the home of friends, the Lindseys. Before she left, Nadean said to her, "It's been nice not seeing you. I haven't been down here. You haven't seen me."

Dolores Finn later described what happened after Sadie left. As the discussion turned into an argument and then into a row, two visitors arrived at the front door. They were Thomas Lindsey and Gerry Reynolds, friends of Paul Dolan. Someone went to talk to them and persuaded them to go away, but while they were on the doorstep they heard enough to convince them that something wasn't quite right inside the house.

They turned back to their car and drove at once to the home of the local community warden, Police Officer Vernon Barnes. With commendable determination to do his duty, even early in the morning on a public holiday, Barnes drove up to see Paul Dolan.

"What's going on?" Barnes asked him. "I've had a report that there's some kind of trouble here."

"It's nothing at all," Dolan assured him. "Just a little argument. It's all over now."

Barnes had no reason to disbelieve him. These things happened on public holidays, he reasoned to himself. He noted the unusual Cadillac parked outside the front door, and then drove back to his home to eat his breakfast.

Meanwhile, in the living-room, Cindy Baillie was shaking with fright, aware that her kidnappers were talking about taking her away to kill her. "I'm not going anywhere," she sobbed. "If you're going to kill me, you'll have to kill me right here."

Nadean then said: "All right. If that's the way you want it." Then she said to Greg: "Hand me that pillow."

Cindy was now in hysterics. "Save me, Greg!" she implored. "Don't let her kill me!"

For answer, Greg tossed the pillow to his mother, aware that Nadean intended to fire through it to prevent blood blowback.

(Blowback is a term used to describe what happens to a human body struck by a bullet. Blood, flesh and body fluids erupt from the impact in the direction from which the bullet came).

"Nadean started teasing Cindy with the gun," Dolores recalled later. "Cindy grabbed the pillow to protect herself when Nadean pointed the gun at her head, and when she moved the pillow up to her face, Nadean pointed the gun at her stomach."

Nadean was laughing at the sport of it but, nauseated by it all, Dolores got up to leave the room. As soon as her back was turned, she recalled, the gun went off. This was the first shot, and it went into the back of the armchair where Cindy was sitting. Nadean moved forward to stand over her.

Paul Dolan came running out of the bathroom, where he had been since Barnes's visit, but Nadean swung the gun on him, warning: "Get back and stay out of this!" Cindy's eyes darted from one to the other. She looked terrified.

Dolores by now was out of the door and heading down the corridor. That was when she heard more shots. She looked round and saw Cindy's head "bobble down" as she slipped out of the chair on to the floor. Nadean was standing over Cindy with the pistol.

According to Dolores, Nadean calmly handed the gun to her son and ordered him to reload it. He looked as unperturbed as his mother as he fed bullets into the weapon. Then Nadean began stamping viciously on Cindy's neck – "bouncing up and down on it," was how Dolores described the action. Cindy was still alive. She was whimpering and struggling feebly.

"Greg handed the loaded gun back to Nadean," Dolores continued tearfully. "He told her to go ahead and empty the gun. She got behind Cindy's body and fired two shots into the back of her head."

She fired four more shots into Cindy, and at that point Paul Dolan protested, "If you had to do it, why did you do it here?"

The next few minutes were a kaleidoscope of action. Paul Dolan hurried out of the house. Nadean and Greg tried to stuff Cindy's corpse into a pair of bin-liners. When it wouldn't fit, Nadean dragged it into a bedroom and ordered Dolores to clean the blood off the living-room floor with a towel.

Nadean then placed the gun in Cindy's hand, saying: "There, that'll make it look like suicide...She won't fit in the car. We'll just leave her here. Paul will take care of it."

Paul, it seems, had no such intention. After he fled from his house he met up with his friends Lindsey and Reynolds. He quickly forgot the mayhem he had left behind and the three friends discussed their plans to spend Independence Day together.

Reynolds recalled: "We decided to have a cook-out at my place – Tom Lindsey, Paul Dolan, and me, and our families. Tom and Paul went over to Paul's house to get a grill to cook steaks on."

Lindsey took over: "When we got there the doors were locked and their shades were drawn. Paul didn't have the key. I took a screen off the window and went in and let Paul in by the back door. Then we walked down the hallway.

"That's when we saw the body lying on the bedroom floor. She was real bloody around the throat and she had dark places on her face. I yelled to Paul to get out of the house and we ran to Gerry Reynolds's house."

"They were sick," Reynolds said. "Paul was violently ill lying in the carport."

In something of a panic, Lindsey and Reynolds drove to Police Officer Vernon Barnes's house and banged on his door. For the second time that day the local community warden was to get an urgent call to the Dolan house.

"You'd better come quickly, Vernon!" they shouted. "There's a dead woman up at Paul Dolan's place. Seems like she's just shot herself."

Vernon Barnes pulled on his jacket and drove back to Paul Dolan's. He found Cindy, who he did not know, sprawled on her back across the carpet, grasping the black, pearl-handled .22-calibre revolver. There was a thick smear of blood on her throat. Her chest was riddled with tiny, angry-looking bullet holes. Dried blood crusted her dress front. Dried bloodstains on the carpet leading to her eventual resting-place indicated that she had been dragged across the floor.

Barnes looked closer, and discovered two additional gunshot wounds behind her right ear, plus another puzzling wound in her throat. This was no suicide, he figured. Not even the most determined suicide victim could do all this to herself.

"This is murder," Barnes said. He looked suspiciously at Paul Dolan, then at his watch. It was two hours since he first called at the house, to investigate what had appeared to be a domestic incident. In his estimation, judged from the developing rigidity of the dead body and the coagulation of the blood, two hours would about cover the time since the victim was shot.

"I didn't do it!" Paul Dolan protested.

Barnes asked: "Who is she?"

Dolan told him her name and address, and added that she had been at his house earlier that morning, when he encountered Barnes the first time. However, he insisted, she was then alive.

Barnes afterwards recalled that Dolan seemed reluctant to talk. "I didn't know at the time if his hesitation was because of guilt, or because he was afraid of something."

With none of those present having any idea of what had happened to Cindy Baillie, what puzzled Vernon Barnes most was the pistol in the dead woman's hand. She hadn't committed suicide, but had she been armed prior to her death and involved in some kind of shootout? There were no bullet holes anywhere in the house to support that possibility.

He needed more help, and when he called in state

detectives they focused on Paul Dolan. They reasoned that he had at first lied to Vernon Barnes about everything being all right in his house, and a couple of hours later he suddenly had a dead woman in his bedroom.

Then came a most significant item of evidence, found in the bedroom – the first hint that the killer might not be a male. It was a woman's orange and white striped tank top, splattered with blood. There were no bullet holes in it. Did it, the investigators wondered, belong to Sadie Dolan, Paul Dolan's wife?

"Blowback," said Detective Perry Proctor, examining the garment. "Whoever was wearing this blouse was standing very near the victim, in the direction from which she was shot."

By the early afternoon of that long day, the investigators had accumulated a significant amount of evidence. Foreign hairs had been painstakingly located and preserved from the victim's body and from the blouse on the bed. A bullet – the first that Nadean had fired – was removed from the armchair. Judging from the state of the corpse, they reckoned Cindy Baillie died some time between 7 and 9 a.m. that day.

Dr. Mohammed Merchant, a state pathologist, would later testify that the victim was shot eight times – once in the back, twice in the head, and five times in the left breast. In addition, there was a stab wound in her throat, made by a knife or some other sharp object, thrust upwards to exit in the oral cavity, piercing the tongue.

Thomas Lindsey and Gerald Reynolds told the investigators how alarm bells began to sound for them when they first went to Paul Dolan's house that day. "We heard quarrelling, and we knew that one of the voices belonged to Nadean Smith." They knew Nadean of old. Just the fact that she was inside caused them to panic.

Thomas Lindsey's wife told the detectives: "About 9 o'clock or so Sadie Dolan came over to our place. She said, 'Nadean Smith is up at the house – and they're going to kill that girl.'"

By "they" she meant Nadean, Nadean's son Greg, and a young woman named Dolores Finn. Although Sadie

Dolan wasn't there and couldn't therefore alibi her husband, she could point the finger of guilt away from him and at one, or all three, of the others who were left in the murder house.

Even so, detectives would not at first dismiss Paul Dolan from their list of suspects, especially as he remained reluctant either to confirm or deny the other witnesses' statements. He refused to elaborate beyond the fact that his ex-wife Nadean had come to his house, along with her son Greg, Dolores Finn, and the victim. Suspicion continued to hang over him, in the words of one investigator, "like smoke over a wet fire."

But by the middle of the day it was obvious that one of the people left in the house that morning had executed Cindy Baillie in cold blood, after arriving at the crime scene in a Cadillac. Where were the trio now? An alert was radioed to the police at Tahlequah, where it was thought they all lived. That proved to be a correct assumption, for the Tahlequah Police knew Lois Nadean Smith very well indeed.

"Meanest damned woman in all of Oklahoma," one officer commented. He cited several cases in which she had been involved in barroom fights and disturbances. On at least one occasion, he said, she had drawn a gun and threatened to use it.

"Nadean Smith is real mean," Detective Mike Daffin confirmed later. "She's a bully. I've never seen so many grown men afraid of one woman."

During the hectic couple of hours that followed, the investigators delved into the lives and backgrounds of the Smiths, mother and son, and of Dolores Finn and Paul Dolan. They were to be reminded that things are seldom clear-cut in a murder case, for several motives surfaced during their inquiries. Their problem was that each motive pointed to a different suspect.

Greg Smith did it, if one believed an informant who told the police that Cindy Baillie had phoned a hit-man on the evening before the murder and offered to pay him an undisclosed sum of money if he would kill Greg Smith. No one seemed to know why Cindy would do this. Greg had found out about the arrangement, the caller said, and intended to kill her before she could have him killed.

Lois Nadean Smith did it, if one believed another anonymous caller, who said that Cindy had turned police informer against Nadean and Greg because of their involvement in narcotics. Other acquaintances of the group insisted that Nadean had killed Cindy because Cindy had become pregnant by Greg.

Dolores Finn did it, if one listened to other witnesses. They would testify at the forthcoming trial that Greg Smith had been having an affair with both Cindy Baillie and Dolores Finn. This had led to jealousy between the two women.

One of the witnesses later claimed in court that Dolores Finn had phoned her shortly after returning from Gans on Independence Day, telling her that killing Cindy had been necessary because Cindy stood in the way of her happiness with Greg.

The only one who didn't seem to have a motive for murdering Cindy was Paul Dolan. As far as Assistant District Attorney Mike Daffin and most of the investigators were concerned, *everyone* in the house that morning should be held at least partially responsible for what happened. But the law wouldn't see it that way. All that the law wanted to know was who pulled the trigger eight times.

It was time, the law decided, to bring in the trio of suspects.

At 3 p.m. in Tahlequah that afternoon, not far from the sprawling campus of Northeastern State University, Officer Albert Penson spotted a copper-coloured Cadillac parked in the street in front of the rundown little house he knew to be the home of the woman everyone called the town's notorious female bully, currently wanted for questioning as a murder suspect.

Officer Penson radioed for backup before attempting to approach the house or the car. Two more patrolmen responded, and the three officers entered the house and surprised Nadean Smith, who was partly drunk, and

Greg in the living-room. They offered no resistance.

Shortly after they were arrested, other officers found Dolores Finn at her home. The three were escorted to the sheriff's office in Sallisaw for questioning, while lab experts examined the Cadillac for any evidence that might link its occupants to the crime scene. They found nothing.

Assistant DA Daffin later described the arrival of the Smiths and Dolores Finn at the sheriff's office. "The girl Dolores was quiet and withdrawn. She looked frightened. But Nadean and Greg – they really put on an act."

"What's going on here?" the mother and son demanded. "We don't know what you're talking about. We haven't even been in Gans."

Daffin recalled: "Both of them were arrogant and abusive. I conferred with Sheriff Lockhart and Detective Kevin Ottwell, and we eventually agreed that the only person who would give us the time of day was Dolores Finn."

The Smiths were placed in holding cells while Dolores was questioned further. Minutes later tears were welling in her eyes as she unburdened herself of the terrible events that began at dawn and culminated in the brutal, cold-blooded murder in the living-room of Paul Dolan's home.

Finally she recalled that as the three of them pulled down the window shades after the murder and locked the doors before leaving. Nadean had cautioned Dolores that she would be the next to die if she told anyone about the crime. "I – I was scared to death. I didn't know what to do, because I knew Nadean meant what she said."

But as he filed first-degree murder charges against the Smiths, Daffin knew that the case was by no means open and shut. The police believed that Dolores had told the truth, but Nadean and Greg were saying nothing, except to profess their innocence.

As the investigation continued over the next few days, detectives learned that the Smiths proposed to blame Dolores for the murder, claiming she shot Cindy during a bitter quarrel over Greg Smith. Several witnesses surfaced who would support this. One of them was Paul Dolan.

According to the testimony that Gerald Reynolds would later give the jury, Paul Dolan was to explain away the disturbance at his house that morning before the body was found by insisting that the group "was just roughing up Cindy Baillie. Pulling her hair, and things like that." Dolan had also told Reynolds that he had talked Greg Smith out of killing the girl, but then Dolores spoke up: "We have to go ahead – it's my ass, too."

Several other witnesses were prepared to support the Smiths, describing the intense jealousy between Dolores and Cindy.

Nadean and Greg's plot to transfer guilt from themselves to Dolores, who was being held as a material witness to murder and who was already identified as the state's "star witness," emerged when the authorities intercepted a jailhouse note from Nadean, intended for her son. The note instructed Greg about what his testimony should be.

"*Read this over and over till you learn what to say,*" the note read. "*Don't let anyone see you with it. Flush down toilet when finished.*

"*Dolores put gun in Cindy's hand. Me and you never touched gun. Dolores pulled Cindy...bedroom.*

"*I didn't stomp on her throat. Dolores did, if we are asked.*

"*You have got to say that me and you...heard two or three shots, ran out in the hall. Cindy was in her chair, holding knife. Dolores was standing beside her with gun.*

"*I was in...bedroom. You came back in...We heard three or four shots and went into living-room and Cindy was laying on floor on her back. Dolores was standing with gun.*

"*We did not help clean up blood. Don't know where gun came from. I did not once have gun...*

"*Dolores and Cindy were fussing. Dolores had been taking pills and drinking beer.*

"*I did not try to choke her coming from the motel.*

"*Dolores was very jealous of you. I was never fussing with no one. Dolores asked Cindy to go to Gans with us... "*

Mike Daffin had an uneasy feeling that the plot might succeed and the Smiths be freed by a jury unless the investigators could produce sufficient evidence to counter the Smiths' claims.

Detectives next found to their surprise that it was Cindy Baillie herself who bought the death weapon from a pawnshop in Tahlequah a few weeks previously. However, a friend of Cindy's explained that Cindy had loaned the gun to Greg Smith in June and Greg had refused to return it to her. Greg still had the gun on Independence Day, the day of the murder.

The state medical examiner dispelled all the rumours that Cindy had been killed because she was pregnant. His examination of the body showed that she was not.

This of course ran counter to Cindy's own assertion, when she asked to be killed quickly because she was expecting a baby and was fearful for it. Was she hoping for sympathy, or did she mistakenly believe that she was pregnant?

Ballistics experts confirmed that the victim had been shot with the .22 pistol found in her hand. Other experts concluded that hair specimens recovered from the dead body and the bloody blouse found at the crime scene belonged to Nadean Smith. But the most remarkable piece of detective work came from a forensic chemist, Kenneth Ead, who was to add the final touch to the proof that Nadean Smith had pulled the trigger.

Other experts had already linked Nadean to the blouse. They could prove that it was hers. It was Ead who demonstrated that the person who wore the blouse was also the person who fired the fatal shots. Using an elaborate system of experiments, he showed by comparing angles that the blowback that stained the blouse matched precisely the angle of the bullet wounds in Cindy's body.

"In other words," said Prosecutor Daffin, "Nadean either killed Cindy, or someone had to stand directly behind Nadean and reach round her to do the shooting."

Although no firm motive for the crime had been established, Daffin was satisfied with the investigation and was prepared to take the case to court.

On November 12th, 1982, defence lawyers successfully applied for separate trials for their clients. Lois Nadean Smith went on trial first, on December 6th. With the heavyweight evidence of Dolores Finn stacked against her, she was found guilty of first-degree murder 12 days later.

While the press stridently attacked "the meanest woman in all Oklahoma," her lawyer argued eloquently against the death penalty. He pleaded: "Give her, under your verdict, whatever this woman has never had before. Give her the freedom to read, to be creative, to find herself. Give her the day to day opportunity to exist in whatever she is allowed, or chooses, to involve herself in."

But Prosecutor Daffin insisted that Nadean Smith deserved no mercy. Cindy's murder, he said, was "heinous, atrocious and cruel." Nadean had shown no compassion for the pleas of her frightened victim, whom she had tortured and then gunned down.

"There have been many tears shed during this trial," he added, alluding to outbursts by the defendant and her witnesses. "But no one cries for Cindy Baillie."

The jury recommended the death penalty, and on December 29th, 1982, Judge Bill Ed Rogers sentenced her to die by lethal injection.

At his subsequent trial Greg Smith was convicted of murder and given a life sentence.

Due to the almost interminable appeals process, his mother eluded the death chamber until she was 61. By then, however, she was "ready to go home," said a prison spokesman. "She's glad she's almost done with this."

Her victim's daughter, Brandy Fields, who was four when her mother was murdered, commented: "Lois Nadean Smith has had the privilege of breathing for 20 years too long."

It later emerged that even at high school Nadean Smith was known as "Mean Nadean." But the now apparently contrite killer issued a statement. "To the family, I want to say I'm sorry for all the pain I caused you. Please forgive me."

Nadean Smith was executed at Oklahoma State Penitentiary on Tuesday, December 4th, 2001. Among those who came to watch was Brandy Fields. Referring to Nadean's statement of contrition she said, "I wish she'd thought about this before she did it. If she had, we wouldn't be here right now. You do something of this magnitude, torturing someone, and you're going to have to pay the price for it. She chose her path in life."

Brandy's father, Bill Whitson, compared Nadean to Osama Bin Laden, maintaining that some people needed to die for what they had done.

For Whitson, Nadean's remorse was 19 years too late. "There hasn't been a peep out of her for the last 19 years saying I'm sorry," he said. "If there's no apology after all that time, there's no repentance. She's the same person now that she was 19 years ago."

Nadean Smith's last meal, at her request, was barbecued ribs, onion rings, strawberry banana cake and cherry limeade. After that she was taken to the death chamber, given a lethal injection, and was pronounced dead at 9.13 p.m.

Greg Smith, now in his 40s, is still in prison. He didn't attend the execution of the woman whose fiercely protective mother-love put him behind bars for life. And if Brandy Fields has her way, he'll never be released. "I still have to go to parole hearings, so it's not completely over," she says. "I'll have to go and do that until he dies."

When Oklahoma executed Lois Nadean Smith the state had put to death more women in one year than any other state since 1866. Before 2001 Oklahoma had not executed a woman since pre-statehood days. Dora Wright, 39, was hanged in 1903 for murdering a young girl from Wilburton. The chart on pages 93 and 94 shows that in the years 1935, 1944 and 1953, three women were executed in each year, but not from the same state.

So does Oklahoma have a tougher policy on the

execution of women? No, said the state's attorney-general, explaining that before the execution of Wanda Jean Allen on January 11th, 2001, a woman had not been executed in Oklahoma in modern times because none of their cases had progressed that far. It simply hadn't been their turn yet, he said.

"Gender is simply not relevant to the legal process. But of course whenever you have someone of a different gender or background they tend to attract more attention."

Nonetheless, in 2002 Oklahoma executed 18 men and women, more than any other state, and that includes Texas. It's a fact that suggests its policy on capital punishment has at least hardened.

6 – LESBIAN KILLED SEVEN MEN IN A YEAR
Aileen Wuornos

Slowly, indistinctly, enlightenment filtered through to the Florida homicide detectives – the serial killer they were looking for was a woman.

They could be forgiven for having been puzzled up till now. After all, it wasn't every day they were tracking the killer of seven middle-aged men, and it was even more rare to be on the trail of a vicious woman murderer. In fact, they had never had one in the state before.

But the clues were there before their eyes. All the victims were shot in the chest – a classic target for a woman killer, who will rarely fire at her victim's head. All the victims' abandoned vehicles were found with the driver's seat pushed well forward. And one of them contained a long blonde hair.

"She must be a crazy hooker," one of the officers suggested. "A hitch-hiker who robs and kills as soon as she's picked up."

She was even more than that. She was a lesbian with a deeply ingrained hatred of men. Not just for the men who used her as a prostitute, it seemed, but for the masculine gender in general.

She was 46-year-old Aileen Wuornos, and she went to the electric chair as philosophically as she had announced to the police that she had killed six middle-aged men who picked her up for sex. "I am a serial killer and I would kill again," she said. "All I wanna do is go to the chair and get off this planet, which is full of evil."

Aileen's killing spree began in the autumn of 1989 and was all over by the autumn of 1990 – a 12-month period in which she killed six times. Her first victim was Richard Mallory, a 56-year-old video store owner who picked her up while he was driving to Daytona on business on November 30th, 1989.

When his naked body was found a fortnight later investigators suspected he had become the victim of someone he had picked up, but they were puzzled by the ferocity of the attack. He had been shot in the arm, leg, and several times in the chest, and when his car was found it had been wiped clean of fingerprints.

David Spears, a 43-year-old construction worker, was the second victim, He disappeared on May 19th, 1990, and his body was discovered 16 days later in wasteland 40 miles north of Tampa. Like Richard Mallory's, his corpse was naked and he had been shot several times in the chest with a .22 pistol His pickup truck was found abandoned off Interstate Highway 75, about 20 miles south of Gainesville.

The third nude corpse of a man was found two days later on June 6th, again off Interstate 75. The victim had been shot nine times with .22-calibre bullets, and he was identified as Charles Carskaddon, 41, who vanished on May 31st while driving to Tampa to pick up his fiancée.

Body number four was that of 46-year-old Troy Burress, a lorry driver missing since July 30th. He was found by picnickers in Oscala National Park on August 4th, shot in the chest and the back by a .22 weapon. His lorry had been discovered abandoned four days earlier.

Scrubland off Interstate 75 near Falmouth yielded up body number five on September 12th. It was the remains of Richard Humphreys, a 56-year-old retired police chief. His car had been stolen, and he had been shot seven times in the chest with a .22 handgun.

By this time investigators had deduced that the killer was a woman and, as the victims were all motorists, a hitchhiking hooker was suspected.

Florida had never had a female serial killer before, but the investigators' scenario began to seem increasingly convincing. The victims would have stopped voluntarily for a woman, either for sex or to give her a lift, expecting no danger from a female.

A sixth body, that of Walter Gino Antonio, a 60-year-old ex-cop, was discovered on November 19th in Dixie County. His corpse was virtually naked, like those of Mallory, Spears and Carskaddon, and he had multiple .22 bullet wounds.

The trail that led detectives to Aileen Wuornos involved a seventh motorist. He was Peter Siems, a 65-year-old missionary. His body has never been found, but on July 4th, 1990, witnesses saw two women abandon his car after it took a bend too fast and left the road.

Several people who saw the incident rushed to help the two women. But they refused all offers and hurried away from the scene on foot.

"One was a blonde, the other a sort of dumpy redhead," the witnesses told police, who became interested when they found Peter Siems's blood on the car's front seat.

An artist's impression of the two women, based on the witnesses' descriptions, was sent to police throughout Florida and shown on television. This brought in a number of responses, and suspicion focused on two lesbians. They were Tyria Moore, a thickset redhead, and fair-haired Cammie Marsh Green, who had been living together at a Port Orange motel.

Cammie Green was a prostitute also known as Lee Blahovee. When a photo of her was shown to the motel's woman owner she recognised her as one of the two women who had left the place recently.

Shown a photo of sixth victim Gino Antonio's car, found abandoned on November 24th, the motel owner then identified it as the vehicle she had seen Cammie Green driving during her stay.

Next, a check on pawn shops in the area revealed that Cammie Green had recently pawned a camera belonging to Richard Mallory, her first victim, and a toolbox belong to David Spears, victim number two. One of the pawn tickets bore her thumbprint – and that print identified her by her real name as Aileen Wuornos, 34 years old, whose criminal record stretched right back into her childhood.

On January 8th, 1991, detectives spotted her outside a bar in Port Orange, Florida. They kept her under surveillance until the next day, when she was arrested at the aptly named Last Resort bar in nearby Harbor Oaks. The charge at this point was merely a pretext, involving having a concealed weapon.

Tyria Moore, 29, was traced to Pennsylvania. Frightened by media reports of the police hunt for two women wanted for six murders, she had deserted the lesbian lover she knew to be the killer, and now she turned out to be eager to talk.

"I wasn't involved in killing anyone," she stressed. "I only heard about Mallory's murder when Aileen and me were sittin' around and talkin', and she jest came right out of the blue and said she had somethin' to tell me, and she told me she had shot and killed a man right on that very same day.

"She told me she's shot and killed this guy Richard Mallory. She said she hid his body in the woods under a bit of old carpet she's found in his car. I asked her what she's done with the car and she said, 'I got rid of it. I jest walked away from it.'

"She had a box with all this guy Mallory's personal stuff in it. She took a picture out of the box and showed it to me. She said, 'This is a picture of the guy I shot.'"

Mindful that Aileen had several times in the past said she hated men because they had abused her, a detective asked Tyria: "Did she explain why she had shot him? Did she tell you, for instance, that she had been beaten and raped? Did she show any remorse?"

"The answer to all those questions," Tyria replied, "is no."

Why didn't Tyria go to the police? "I was just scared," she claimed. "She always said she'd never hurt me, but then you can't believe her, so I jest don't know what she would've done."

The detectives checked Tyria's story and found she was at work at the time of some of the murders. In return for an assurance that she would not be prosecuted for complicity, she agreed to help with the investigation. She was flown back to Daytona Beach, where she was installed in a motel, and when Aileen phoned her from jail Tyria told her that she herself would soon be behind bars unless Aileen owned up and confessed to everything.

In the tape-recorded phone call, on January 16th,

1991, Aileen replied: "If I have to confess just to keep you from getting into trouble, I will. You know how much I love you. I will not let you be involved in the picture. You're not the one. I'm the only one. I'm the one who did everything. I did it all by myself. You were at work every time I did one."

Three days later Aileen confessed to all six murders with which she was charged. As for the missing missionary, Peter Siems, she told detectives that she had dumped his body in a swamp. But despite a long search it never came to light.

In each case, she said, she had shot the victim to stop him trying to rape her, beat her, or "screw me in the ass."

Why didn't she just keep them at bay with her pistol? "Once I got my gun," she said, "I was like, hey, man, I gotta shoot you, 'cause I think you're gonna kill me. See?"

So why had she shot them so many times and not just once? "I was afraid that if I shot 'em one time and they survived, my face and all that description of me would be all over the place."

And why did she steal their possessions? "That was out of pure hatred."

Told that Tyria Moore was to end their four-year relationship by betraying her, Aileen claimed: "She was my pimp and I was her white slave. She wanted money and clothes and a place to live. She would tell me, 'Go out there and work.' If I didn't she would break up with me and find another girl who would definitely take care of her. I did it because I loved her to the max."

Even so, Tyria's sudden departure from the motel where they shared a bedroom had devastated her. Unable to live with the memories, Aileen herself left the motel and took to sleeping on an old car seat outside the Last Resort bar, drowning her sorrows in drink she paid for by selling her favours.

Suddenly she was overwhelmed with remorse. The killings were preying on her mind, she said. She felt she deserved to die and wanted to be "right with God."

The police told the media that she was a cold-blooded killer whose methods were practical and efficient. She would set out to look for a victim, taking with her a bag of clothes in case those she was wearing became bloodstained, a bottle of household cleaner to remove fingerprints, and a seven-shot .22 revolver, since recovered from a river where she had dumped it.

"She set out deliberately to rob, and killed her victims so they couldn't identify her," said Police Sergeant Bruce Munster.

Aileen didn't agree with all of that. Although she admitted the murders, she denied planning them. At her first court hearing she said the motorists were her clients. She had sex with at least three a day, four days a week, and at busy seasons she would pick up 40 or 50 men in a week and earn as much as $1,000.

She said she hadn't intended to kill Richard Mallory, but he tied her to the steering wheel and raped her. "He put a cord around my neck," she told the court, "and he said, 'You will do everything I tell you to do, because if you don't I'll kill you just like all the other sluts I've done.'"

She said he then lifted her legs over his shoulders and raped her anally. "It really hurt because he tore me up bad. I was screaming in pain, but he was saying he loved hearing about my pain because it turned him on."

When she managed to reach her handbag that contained her gun, "I shot him as fast as I could."

Aileen's trial for Richard Mallory's first-degree murder began on Monday, January 13th, 1992. Her defence lawyers claimed that her years as a prostitute had pushed her to the brink of insanity. She had been brutalised so often, they said, that when Mallory attacked her she snapped.

It was a claim that might have hit the nail on the head, so to speak, for the police knew that Mallory had served 10 years for a ferocious rape. This was never mentioned during the trial. And the judge decided to admit the evidence of the six other killings – a decision that inevitably prejudiced the jury.

Both Mallory's widow and a former lover of his testified in support of Aileen, describing in vivid terms his violence towards them. But her credible self-defence story was undermined by Tyria Moore's story and the cold-blooded logic of the prosecutor.

He told the jury: "Common sense says that a person is not going to have to use deadly force to kill another human being in self-defence seven times in one year.

"A police officer on the street every day, dealing with criminals, doesn't have to kill seven people in a year. Most policemen don't kill one person in a lifetime. Yet the defence want you to believe that she ran into seven men within one year and had to kill them all."

It sounded good – but does it come out quite so good when you analyse it? In strict legal terms, Aileen was tried for killing one man, Richard Mallory. She claimed that he tied her up and raped her, which might cause some to say, well, she would say that, wouldn't she?

But Mallory was exactly the type of man who would have done just that. Two women testified to his brutality, and he had already done a stretch of 10 years for violent rape. In all the circumstances, at least under Federal law she would have been perfectly entitled to kill him.

As for the other six victims, Aileen readily testified that she picked up 40 or 50 men a week in busy seasons, which might be up to 2,000 men in a year. Might a mere six of those 2,000 have been of the Richard Mallory type? If so, was she not in part driven to her extreme self-defence?

Of course, she went armed, and with a change of clothes, ready to kill if necessary, and that makes her highly suspect. But if she did pick up as many as 2,000 men a year, 1,994 walked free from her embrace – in other words they paid for their sex and didn't beat her up.

The prosecutor's analogy with a policeman should have been savaged by the defence. A policeman doesn't encounter the likelihood of extreme danger with everyone he encounters, whereas a prostitute does, and mentally prepares herself for it.

But none of these considerations washed with the jury. They found her guilty. The trial's penalty phase ended with them having no sympathy at all for Aileen. They recommended the death penalty, which the judge affirmed on January 31st, 1992.

Aileen Wuornos erupted in fury. "I was raped! I hope you get raped, scumbags of America!" she screamed at the jury's women members.

She protested: "I've been labelled a serial killer, and I'm no serial killer. I've been framed by law enforcement. I was not out there to hurt anyone. I was raped or beaten thirty-nine times. What I did was what anyone else would do. I defended myself."

Two months later she sacked her lawyers and engaged a new team to represent her. They weren't of much help. They persuaded her to change her not guilty plea to one of "no contest" to the remaining murder charges. This was tantamount to admitting the murders, and the pleas of no contest, according to her lawyer, were entered so that she could fulfil her wish to die in the electric chair.

She was subsequently given five more death sentences, but although she had now apparently got what she wanted, her mood was highly changeable She repeated her claim that she had killed only in self-defence, and probably didn't endear herself to the judiciary when she told the judge: "I hope your wife and children get raped – in the ass!"

By 2001 she wanted to change her lawyers again. One of them, who contested her bid to sack him, said she didn't understand the ramifications of what she was doing, and her behaviour raised questions about her mental health. In other words, she needed protecting from herself

Lawyers from the state agency that handles death sentence appeals announced that they would try to have her declared incompetent.

The sister of one of her victims, the lorry driver Troy Burress, pleaded to Aileen to end her appeals. "I don't hate her," she said, "I hate what she did." Burress's daughter said it was time for the appeals to end, and they should not be allowed to drag on.

Aileen at last agreed with her. In July, 2001, she told a court hearing: "I am a serial killer and I would kill again. I want to clear all the lies and let the truth come out. I have hate crawling through my system."

Judge Michael Hutcheson said he would recommend to the Florida Supreme Court that she was competent to make the decision she wanted. "But that will put you on the fast track to execution," he warned her.

Aileen replied: "I'm not scared by it. I know what the heck I'm doing."

At her original trial in 1992 she had claimed that her victims had assaulted her and made her fear for her life. But now she said she had lied. "I killed those men in the first degree, robbed them and killed them."

Apologising to their families, she said there was no point in wasting more taxpayers' money on her defence. There was no sense in it. "The world doesn't mean anything to me."

In April, 2002, the Florida Supreme Court agreed that Aileen Wuornos was mentally competent to drop her appeals, and after that there was nothing left but for Florida state governor, Jed Bush, brother of George W. to sign the death warrant.

Five months later, on October 9th, she declined the condemned prisoner's traditional last meal, which could have been anything she wanted costing up to $20. Instead, she was given a cup of coffee.

By now Florida had stopped using the electric chair in favour of lethal injection, so at 9.30 a.m., in the execution chamber at Florida's State Penitentiary, the process began of injecting lethal drugs into her arms. A brown curtain was drawn back, and witnesses saw her turn to them, pull a bizarre face, give a kind of grin, roll her eyes and turn away. Strapped so that she was able to move only her head, she shut her eyes at 9.31 and her head jerked forward. A minute later, her mouth appeared to drop open, and at 9.47 the 46-year-old serial killer was pronounced dead.

Asked minutes earlier if there were anything she

wished to say, she replied: "Yes, I would just like to say I'm sailing with the Rock (Jesus), and I'll be back, like Independence Day with Jesus, June 6th, like the movie, big mother ship and all. I'll be back, I'll be back."

7 – WAS GREAT-GRANNY'S EXECUTION AN ELECTION STUNT?
Betty Lou Beets

"I'm asking you to let me live. I'm asking for mercy."

These were the words of Betty Lou Beets, a 62-year-old great-grandmother, and they were addressed to the then governor of Texas, George W. Bush. Would they have moved him?

On the downside against Granny Beets was the fact that she had spent a lot of her life surrounded by self-made mayhem. But it had to be a point in her favour that she was a battered wife. It certainly complicated the situation. If Bush ordered a stay of execution he would be accused of going soft, but if he gave the go-ahead he would be condemned for supporting the execution of an abused wife.

And that, it was thought, could jeopardise his ambitions to become president of the United States.

The trouble that put Betty Lou Beets on Death Row began when the police became curious about the disappearance of her fifth husband. Captain Jimmy Don Beets of the Dallas Fire Department had been married to her for only 11 months in August, 1983, when she reported him missing.

They were living in her mobile home at Cherokee Shores on Cedar Creek Lake when she called the police. "My husband went fishing this morning," she said. "It's now gone midnight and he still hasn't come home."

His motorboat was found drifting on the lake the next day. The drive was out of the water and the propeller was missing. His spectacles lay in the boat, together with an open tool kit and a bottle that had contained the nitro-glycerine tablets that he carried for a slight heart complaint.

It seemed that some submerged object had sheared off his boat's propeller-pin, and while removing the propeller to fit a new pin he'd had a heart attack and toppled into the water.

The lake was dragged without finding him, and a month later one of his friends went to the police to voice his suspicions.

"Jimmy Don hadn't needed his tablets for more than a year, and he used his glasses only for reading," the friend said. "On the boat he would have had them in his pocket and they would have gone overboard with him. He wouldn't have needed them to fix the propeller.

"And there's something else. He's just had a medical check-up and he was found to be in a tip-top condition. He was also a very strong swimmer."

Detectives listening to this story were impressed. And when the friend added darkly: "You know, she divorced her previous husband – he was the fourth one – after he too disappeared without trace," they decided to look more deeply into the married life of Betty Lou Beets.

Questioned by police, she said that she couldn't understand why Jimmy Don's body had not been found in the lake. Her previous husband, she said, had simply walked out on her and she had not heard from him since.

Her first marriage had produced five children, ending in divorce 13 years later. She had been charged with attempting to murder her second husband, and her claim that she had acted in self-defence was unconvincing because he was shot twice in the back while fleeing from her apartment. He had refused to testify against her, however, so the charge was reduced to aggravated assault, for which she was fined $100.

After this second husband's death from a heart attack she married a third, who vanished shortly afterwards and was never found. The fourth husband, Doyle Wayne Barker, had owned the mobile home where she still lived, and which was awarded to her after she sued for divorce on grounds of his desertion.

No one had heard that Barker intended to leave her, and no one heard from him after he left.

Barker worked for a building contractor. One day in November, 1981, he failed to turn up for work. At the end of that week Betty Lou went to the firm to collect his back pay. She said they'd had a row and he'd gone off.

Now she was petitioning to have her fifth husband declared legally dead so that she could collect his $100,000 life insurance, his property, and a $792-a-month pension as a fireman's widow.

Betty Lou's matrimonial history suggested that she must be at least unlucky in marriage. Dame Fortune didn't seem to smile too favourably on most of her husbands, either.

Looking round her home, investigators learned that shortly after Captain Jimmy Don moved in with her as husband number five she got him to cover part of her small garden with concrete and erect a shed on it.

Then she got him to dig her a wishing-well. He disappeared before it could be filled with water, and so she filled it with earth in which she planted petunias.

For the hardened Dallas cops that sounded interesting. They got a search warrant and began digging. Pretty soon they found Captain Jimmy Don's body buried in the filled-in well, and the remains of husband number four, Doyle Barker, under the concrete. Both had been shot twice in the head.

Charged with the first-degree murder of both husbands, Betty Lou Beets was tried only for the second killing. She claimed that her son, who was staying with them, shot Captain Jimmy Don accidentally. As her son was on probation she knew the police would never believe him, so she had decided to "take care of it" for him.

But the court heard damning evidence from two of her relatives who were both granted immunity from prosecution. A woman relative testified that Betty Lou had phoned her, saying she was tired of the continual verbal and physical abuse she was taking from Barker, and she was going to kill him.

"I told her not to talk silly," the witness said. "If she couldn't get along with him, she should get a divorce." Betty Lou replied that would leave her without a roof over her head.

The next day Betty Lou told the witness she waited

until Barker went to bed and was asleep. "She told me she put a pillow over his head and shot him twice in the head."

Betty Lou added that she had already started to dig Barker's grave in the garden. After shooting him she completed the digging and buried him.

The next witness was her 21-year-old son, who said he was at Betty Lou's home when she told him to "get lost" for a while because she was going to kill her husband Captain Jimmy Don. He testified that he rode around on his motorbike for a couple of hours, and when he returned Jimmy Don's body lay in a sleeping bag outside the back door of the mobile home.

"Betty Lou asked me to help her drag it around the front. We put it in the wishing-well and then covered it with dirt."

Then they went to the lake, where Betty Lou told him to take the propeller of Captain Jimmy Don's boat off the drive unit while she scattered his heart pills on the floor of the vessel. That done, they pushed the boat out on to the lake.

Why hadn't the witness gone to the police, he was asked? He replied that he felt duty-bound to protect Betty Lou by keeping quiet about the incident because she was his mother.

Giving evidence on her own behalf, Betty Lou declared: "I would never hurt Jimmy Don. No one was ever as good to me as he was. I loved him very much."

In his concluding speech the prosecutor told the jury that Betty Lou was lying when she claimed that Captain Jimmy Don was shot accidentally. He had been shot twice in the back of the head.

Convicted of her fifth husband's murder, Betty Lou Beets was sentenced to die by lethal injection. Then she began to tell different stories about her relationship with Beets and Barker. Both husbands had battered her, she claimed. And in an interview she said she was raped at the age of five by her father and physically abused by men throughout her life.

From her death cell she wrote: "I really believe that to

kill me is to tell every battered woman that there is not a chance, that there is no end but death, that we can't fight back."

Her daughter, Fay Lane, claimed: "I've seen her beaten up by her husbands so many times I can't remember." And according to her lawyer, Betty Lou's "lifetime of abuse" had resulted in brain damage, post-traumatic stress disorder, battered woman's syndrome and rape-trauma syndrome.

How much of all this was true, and how much of it was a specially contrived escape route from Death Row? Well, it also emerged that Betty Lou Beets had been a foul-mouthed barmaid popular with customers because of her ability to talk dirty, and that she also had a reputation as a shrill-voiced harridan who was often heard berating her husbands.

The truth is, she probably gave as good as she got and possibly some more, and so long as there was the death penalty she seemed to be as good a candidate for it as any, regardless of her age and sex.

"If Betty Lou did feel like she was abused, and that's a big if, she could have walked away," said one of Jimmy Don's sons from an earlier marriage. "She didn't have to shoot a guy in the back of the head as he was sleeping."

Nevertheless, her impending fate placed Texas governor George W. Bush in an awkward position. He claimed to be "compassionate conservative," a description that would contrast strangely with sending to the death chamber the oldest woman ever to be executed in the United States, a woman with nine grandchildren and six great-grandchildren.

Bush, who was determined to be the next president of the United States, had notched up an impressive record of judicial killings – 120 of them, all of them legal, all watched by numerous witnesses and all applauded by the voters who elected him governor of Texas, which executes more prisoners than any other state.

As the state's governor he was the man who could order a 30-day reprieve during which the defendant can go back to the courts. But throughout his stewardship as governor, Bush never exercised that right, never made an exception. Although a governor cannot grant clemency, a 30-day stay of execution amounts to much the same thing. It sends a strong message to the state's Pardons and Parole Board, which can commute a death sentence to life imprisonment.

The Texas Pardons and Parole Board was composed of Bush's nominees, and had he ordered a stay of execution in any of the cases referred to him the prisoner's life would have been spared. But reprieves don't win votes, and that's what it's all about. Justice doesn't come into it.

By February, 2000, the furore over the execution of Karla Faye Tucker was largely forgotten when the Betty Lou Beets file landed on the governor's desk. She had by then been 14 years on Death Row, spending most of her time sewing and embroidering. Her plea to the governor, "I'm asking you to let me live," impassioned liberals and brought her case on to the front pages in blazing headlines. Bush was in a dilemma.

Women's rights campaigners were quick to make the most of Betty Lou's supposedly battered history. But, true to form, Bush was more sensitive to right-wing pressure urging him to remain tough on crime. Unwavering in his support for the death penalty, the man who had sanctioned a record number of executions since taking office refused to order a 30-day postponement.

The case even made headlines in London, where the *Daily Mail* darkly predicted, "Death Row case may end Bush's shot at the presidency." It did no such thing, of course – if anything it enhanced it.

"What my husbands started, Texas will finish," Betty Lou said on February 25th, 2000, shortly before she was taken to the death chamber at Huntsville, where she was strapped on a stretcher. She had refused a last meal of her choice.

One of the execution's witnesses said that the great-granny smiled as the lethal chemicals surged through her veins just before she lost consciousness. Her lawyer, however, saw something different. He said she was racked by a spasm, retching as she heaved in a convulsion against the restraining straps across her chest, arms, knees and ankles, and spittle poured from her mouth with her last gasp.

"What happened is not ennobling, and it's not something of which we should be proud," he declared. "It's an act of which we should be deeply ashamed."

Ten minutes after receiving the injection, Betty Lou was pronounced dead. She left behind her five more Texas women awaiting the same fate.

Leaving the death chamber wearing a cowboy hat, one of Doyle Barker's sons told reporters he was "very happy. The state of Texas did the right thing tonight. I want the world to know that there is always going to be a death penalty in the state of Texas."

That was certainly true as far as Governor George W. Bush was concerned. He opposed a bill to prohibit the execution of mentally ill prisoners; he promoted legislation to limit appeals by Death Row inmates; and he supported "speed the juice" moves to cut the time between conviction and execution.

The incompetence of Texas's poorly paid, inadequately trained, court-appointed public defenders is notorious. These are the lawyers chosen to represent prisoners unable to pay for legal aid, and in some cases the defendants would be better off without them. The attorney who defended Betty Lou Beets was an alcoholic subsequently convicted of a felony and struck off, and she later complained that he had failed to present her story of physical abuse in her defence. Another Texas Death Row inmate, Calvin Burdine, had to be released because his attorney at his trial kept falling asleep.

Recognising that its prisoners were getting a raw deal, the state's legislature unanimously agreed improvements. But what happened? Because the proposed reforms would cost money, might indicate "softness" and would not go down well with voters, Governor Bush vetoed them. His opponents found it hard to reconcile this action with his presentation in his presidential campaign as "a reformer with results."

After Betty Lou Beets was put to death, the next Texas prisoner to be executed was Odell Barnes, a 31-year-old black man convicted of raping, beating, stabbing and shooting a woman neighbour to death while robbing her home. His execution provoked a storm of protest as far away as France because his lawyers claimed that the police had planted evidence and had done deals with witnesses to persuade them to give perjured testimony.

The then French president, Jacques Chirac, personally contacted Governor Bush to express his concern that an innocent man had been set up, and a French group that had raised money for Barnes's defence voiced their outrage at his execution. They said: "We consider Bush a serial killer," adding, "This murder will stick like an indelible stain to George W. Bush, who has sacrificed the life of an innocent person for his election."

And Jack Lang, a politician who was bidding to become mayor of Paris, asked: "How can Governor Bush seek to be president of the United States after committing such a crime? Who would listen to demands for the respect of human rights throughout the world from the author of such a barbarous act?"

Odell Barnes himself was more philosophical. Just before his lethal injection was administered on March 2nd, 2000, he expressed his gratitude to his sympathisers for their support. "I thank you for proving my innocence," he said, "although it has not been acknowledged by the courts. Life has not been that good to me, but I believe that now, after meeting so many people who support me in this, that all things will come to an end, and may this be the fruit of better judgments for the future."

In the eyes of the French, Governor Bush was a man with blood on his hands. It should be said that the French consistently held the same view after he became president and ordered the invasion of Iraq.

But in 2000 all the presidential candidates who were vying to succeed Bill Clinton supported the death penalty. America is so firmly wedded to capital punishment that opposing it would be political suicide.

No one was more aware of this than Bill Clinton

himself. During his 1992 campaign to make it to the White House he realised that he had to act tough as governor of Arkansas if he was to win enough votes. So in a move worthy of Governor Bush he declined to order a stay of execution for Ray Rector, a brain-damaged cop-killer so mentally retarded that on Death Row he had become known as "Chicken Man" because he insisted that the guards were tossing chickens into his cell.

Any American politicians accused of lacking compassion, however, can cite a classic example of the folly of being soft. Clemency, they will tell you, can be downright dangerous. Look, for instance, at what happened in 1988.

In that year Michael Dukakis, governor of Massachusetts, was competing for the US presidency against George W. Bush's father. Standing for the Democrats, Dukakis sought to woo Liberal voters by granting a stay of execution to Willie Horton, a convicted murderer and rapist. This led to Horton's reprieve, but he raped again within a week of his release.

Cook-a-hoop, the "we told you so" Republicans launched an advertisement showing a Horton look-alike walking through a revolving door. That finished Michael Dukakis, and George Bush senior became president.

In his memoirs the British hangman Albert Pierrepoint remarked that whether or not a person was executed was "always fundamentally political." Nowhere is this truer than in America, where countless lives have been sacrificed on the altar of political ambition. No one knew this better than Ruby Laffoon, an obscure Kentucky judge until 1926, when he sentenced two black men to be hanged for raping a white woman. This made him so popular that the voters made him the state's governor.

George W. Bush, when he was a state governor, had his sights set even higher, but his recipe for success was much the same: toughness pays.

He was always confident he would become president, and he did. The reason, he said, was that, "I've always demonstrated I can make tough decisions." The ghosts of more than 120 executed prisoners can vouch for that.

Bush's decisions have certainly been tough on them – but they were just what the voters ordered.

8 – MUM WHO KILLED KIDS PLEADED: "LET ME DIE"
Christina Riggs

When Christina Riggs decided to kill herself and her two children she knew exactly how to set about it. She was a nurse at a Little Rock, Arkansas, hospital, well informed about the nature of deadly poisons. One night in November, 1997, she prised open the cabinet where the toxic medicines were stored and bundled a bunch of them into her handbag.

That night she dosed her children with some amitriptyline anti-depressants in a cup of water to make them drowsy, intending to give them a painless death with heart-stopping potassium chloride injections and then to take her own life in the same way.

What she didn't realise was that the potassium chloride had to be diluted before injection. The dose she plunged into five-year-old Justin's neck began to burn his veins, causing him to wake up crying in agony. To ease his pain she gave him a morphine injection and then smothered him with a pillow. His crying woke up two-year-old Shelby, who her mother also smothered.

Then Christina swallowed 28 anti-depressant tablets, injected herself with potassium chloride and lay down to die beside her children.

She was still alive two hours later when her mother, Carol Thomas, arrived at her daughter's home. Carol found her two grandchildren dead in bed, and her daughter unconscious on the floor. Nearby was the note that Christina had left for Shelby's father. It read:

"I can't live like this any more, and I couldn't bear to leave my children behind to be a burden on you or to be separated and raised apart from their fathers and live knowing their mother killed herself."

Christina, 28, was rushed to hospital, revived and questioned by police. They discovered that her mother's act in saving her life had done her no favours. She had unwittingly prolonged the agony of her daughter, who said her sole wish was to join her children.

The events that led to her death were rooted in her troubled history of failed relationships and her life as a single mother. Telling her story on her own Internet website, she came across as the emotionally insecure victim of one man after another.

A series of lovers cheated on her, leaving her holding not just one but two babies. The first child was the result of casual sex with a man she didn't love. A former lover then came back into the picture, proposing marriage and saying he would regard the expected baby as his own. She gave birth to Justin, and the promised marriage followed, producing a daughter, Shelby. But it wasn't wedded bliss. Her husband left her and both filed for divorce.

After the split her husband's promised child-support payments failed to come through. The children had health problems, and Christina, who worked hard at the local hospital, was approaching the end of her tether.

When she recovered from her suicide bid she was charged with the children's murder. So was there some trigger, her supporters wondered, that had driven her into temporary insanity?

Yes, there was, declared both her lawyer and her mother. In April, 1995, Christina was a nurse at the Veterans' Administration Hospital in Oklahoma City when they started bringing in the horribly maimed victims of a bomb explosion in a government building – an explosion in which 165 people died. Christina was among the nurses who treated the victims and as a result she had suffered post-traumatic stress. This, of course, is the great favourite in America's blame and claim culture.

A hospital spokesman played down the assertion. Christina had not been sent to the actual scene of the blast, he said. Evidently her lawyers thought better of it, because her claim that it affected her was not raised at her trial.

When Christina was brought to court at Little Rock in 1998 she pleaded not guilty on grounds of insanity – a far more robust defence than the story of the bomb explosion. Doctors called by her lawyers testified that she had been severely depressed through sexual abuse as a child, a string of failed relationships with men, a shortage of money and a lack of self-esteem because she was fat.

They argued that her depression was so severe at the time of the killings and her attempted suicide that she could not be held responsible for her actions. She was a caring mother who "that night decided that death would be easier than life."

Prosecutor Larry Jegley countered: "She claims she was horribly depressed, she was overweight, she was a single mom and she didn't have enough money. My response to that is, 'Welcome to America.' Plenty of folks are in far worse situations than she was."

The prosecutor claimed that Christina's children had become an inconvenience to her. She had left them locked in their room by themselves for hours while she went out to compete in karaoke contests, and she had planned their deaths for several weeks. With this in mind she had stealthily stolen potassium chloride and morphine from the hospital where she worked.

The jury found her guilty and during the trial's sentencing phase she told them: "I want to die. I want to be with my babies." After several hours' deliberation her wish was granted – the jury recommending that she should die by lethal injection.

Her lawyer, John Wesley Hall, disclosed: "When they read the sentence she said, 'Thank you,' under her breath. Then she squeezed my hand."

"I'm going home to be with my babies," she said as she was led from the court.

Her mother Carol said: "I would not wish life in prison without parole for her." But human rights activists took a different view, claiming that Christina's desire to die confirmed her mental instability.

Her lawyer begged her to file an appeal, and reluctantly she agreed to do so. But she soon withdrew it. "She really just wanted to get it over with," he said later. She was entitled to delay her execution at any time by resuming the appeals process, but she chose not to do so.

Amnesty International and the American Civil Liberties Union asked the state's governor, Mike Huckabee, to intervene. "Christina Riggs deserves compassion, not the executioner's needle," said William Schultz, executive director of Amnesty International USA. "Her stated desire to die should only sharpen, not absolve, the state of Arkansas's duty to show her that compassion."

A spokesman for Governor Huckabee said that he could not grant clemency because Christina had not asked for it, and in January, 2000, a judge ruled that she was mentally competent to make her decision to abandon all avenues of appeal. The Supreme Court affirmed that ruling, and Tuesday, May 2nd was set for Christina's date with the executioner.

She was to become the first woman to be put to death in Arkansas for more than 150 years, and only the fifth to be executed in America since a moratorium on capital punishment was lifted in 1976. The last woman put to death in Arkansas had been Lavinia Burnett, aged about 70. She and her husband Crawford Burnett had got their son John to murder wealthy Jonathan Selby for his money. After the killing John Burnett fled to Missouri, where he was arrested. His parents were also taken into custody. Convicted as accessories, both were publicly hanged in Fayetteville on Saturday, November 8th, 1845, their son following them to the scaffold on Friday, December 26th.

The death chamber of the Arkansas State Penitentiary at Varner was the scene of Christina Riggs's execution.

"This is what I want," she told her lawyer.

"I know," he replied, his eyes red-rimmed.

Carol Thomas, Christina's mother, was faced with a choice no woman would ever wish to have to make. She could either visit her daughter on Death Row or witness her execution. Under Arkansas state law she could not do both because she was related to both the victims and the murderer.

Carol chose to make that last visit to Death Row for a final talk with her daughter in preference to waving goodbye at the execution. After all, she reasoned, there wasn't much you could say to someone as they were about to be executed.

Before the lethal injection was administered Christina made a short statement: "No words can express how sorry I am for taking the lives of my babies. No way can make up for or take away the pain I have caused everyone who knew and loved them. Now I can be with them as I always intended."

She weighed more than 19 stone, and her execution began 18 minutes late because her executioners were unable to find a suitable vein in her arm. She agreed to have the injections in her wrists, and the first needle was inserted at 9.18 p.m.

One of the three drugs injected was potassium chloride – the same heart-stopper she had injected into her two children. After the first shot she spoke her last words before she slipped into unconsciousness: "I love you, my babies."

"This all started with a suicide attempt," said her lawyer, "and that's how it ended – in what is virtually a state-assisted suicide."

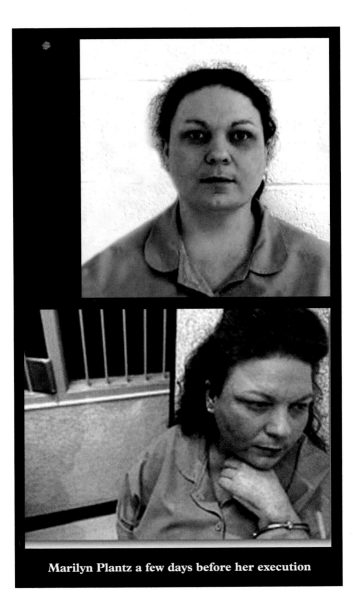

Marilyn Plantz a few days before her execution

Her Husband Was Burned Alive

Lynda Lyon Block displayed no emotion as she was strapped into Alabama's 75-year-old electric chair

A Grudge Against The Whole World

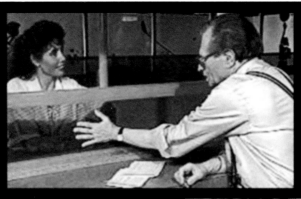

Karla Faye Tucker became the first woman to be executed in Texas since the American Civil War

Pickaxe Double-Murder "Gave Me An Orgasm"

Wanda Jean Allen spent 12 years on Death Row

Before her execution, Lois Nadean Smith finally apologised to the family of her victim

"Don't Let Her Kill Me!"

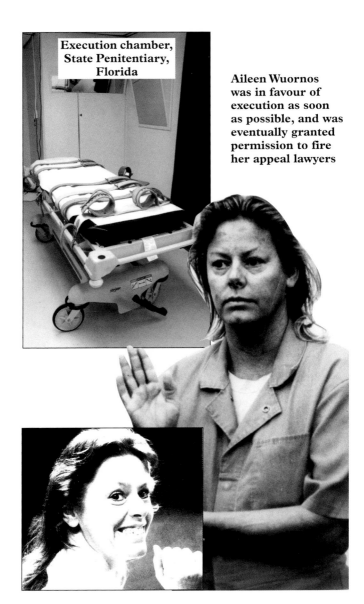

Execution chamber, State Penitentiary, Florida

Aileen Wuornos was in favour of execution as soon as possible, and was eventually granted permission to fire her appeal lawyers

Lesbian Killed Seven Men In A Year

Was Great-Granny's Execution An Election Stunt?

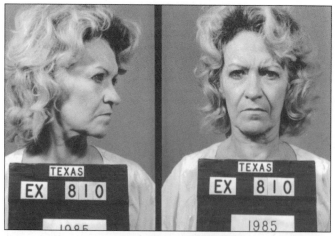

A mugshot of Betty Lou Beets

Christina Riggs intended to kill herself at the same time as taking the lives of her two children

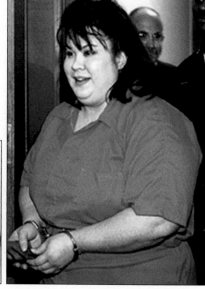

Mum Who Killed Kids Pleaded: "Let Me Die"

Frances Newton claimed she was innocent of the murder of her husband and two children

Lawyer Snoozed While She Fought For Her Life

Martha Beck's last words were: "Let him who is without sin cast the first stone..."

Velma Barfield was the first woman to die by lethal injection

Women Executed In America 1900–2005

9 – LAWYER SNOOZED WHILE SHE FOUGHT FOR HER LIFE
Frances Newton

Frances Newton had good reason to groan inwardly when the court set to try her appointed the lawyer to defend her. He was Ron Mock. He had never won an acquittal in a capital cause, and had lost so many that he was known as "Death Row Mock." His most celebrated claim to fame came about when he fell asleep defending a prisoner who was later executed.

Death Row Mock did nothing to improve his appalling image when he defended Frances Newton. Found guilty, she was sentenced to death.

"I was burned out at the time of her trial," Mock later admitted. "For me it was an uphill battle from the beginning. I had nothing really to work with, other than Frances saying she didn't do it."

In 2001 Mock was finally barred from accepting court-appointed work in capital murder cases. That was much too late for Frances Newton. She had long since died in the electric chair.

Before she died she said: "For a long time I believed in the death penalty, but now I know the system can't be trusted to be right. I've been wrongly accused and wrongly convicted."

Was that the case? Although there are compelling arguments to suggest that she was innocent and did not have a fair trial, that did not seem to be the case in 1988 when Frances, then 22, went on trial in Texas for the killing of her estranged husband and her two children.

It seemed to observers, in fact, that the three murders were so premeditated they wondered how Frances ever thought she might escape detection.

A year before the murders, in March, 1987, she took out $50,000 life insurance policies on herself, her estranged husband Adrian, 23, and their 21-month old daughter Farrah. The life of their seven-year-old son Alton was already insured.

Less than a month later, in the evening of April 7th,

Deputy Sheriff Derek Ricks was called to an apartment complex in West Mount, Houston, where, he was told, there had been a shooting. Frances Newton and her cousin Sondra Nelms were there when the deputy arrived. So too were the bodies of Frances's husband and two children, all shot dead with a .25-calibre pistol.

The police reconstructed the crime, and passed their findings on to the prosecutors. This was the story told at Frances's trial.

Earlier that evening she took her son's blue knapsack out of her car and hid it in an abandoned house owned by her parents. Then she went to cousin Sondra's home next door, and asked her to go with her to Adrian West's apartment in West Mount. They arrived to find Adrian lying on the couch, shot in the head. The children were in their beds, each shot in the chest. Frances promptly called the police.

Deputy Ricks found no signs of forced entry or a struggle at the apartment. Later that evening, a detective interviewed Sondra Nelms. She told him about the blue knapsack she had seen Frances take to the abandoned house. When the police recovered the knapsack, they found it contained a .25-calibre semi-automatic pistol. Ballistics proved it to be the murder weapon.

Two weeks after the killings, Frances filed $100,000 claims on the insurance policies on her husband and daughter. The next day she was arrested and charged with capital murder.

At her trial the evidence against her piled up into a mountain. First, the murder weapon. How did she come by it?

The gun's owner testified hat he had loaned it to his cousin Jeffrey Freelow five or six months before the shootings. Freelow had begun an affair with Frances a month or two prior to the murders, and he identified the pistol, saying he kept it in a chest of drawers in his bedroom.

"Frances had easy access to the chest of drawers because she often did my laundry," he said.

Next, the forensics. An expert testified that he found

nitrates from gunpowder residue on the skirt Frances wore on the day of the shootings. These, he believed, were consistent with the pistol being fired in the lower front area of the skirt.

So what did Frances have to say about all this? "I admit I took the gun to my husband's apartment on the night of the shootings, but it was for protection," she said. "When I left, my husband and the children were alive."

Did she have an explanation for their deaths? "My husband was a long-time drug addict. The family could have been killed by a drug dealer named Charlie as he tried to collect a debt from my husband."

Frances, it turned out, hadn't had a blameless life. A former employer told the court that he'd sacked her for stealing money. And the jury were told that she had been convicted of forgery in 1985 and placed on three years' probation.

After that, the court did not delay. On October 24th, 1988, she was found guilty of capital murder, and the next day she was sentenced to death.

For the next 17 years Frances went through the exhausting appeals procedure. All her efforts were dismissed. But she was not without supporters. She had not had a fair trial, they claimed, and they challenged the evidence against her.

New lawyers were appointed to represent her, and they began by focusing on evidence about a second pistol, claimed to have been found in the abandoned house. This one, they said, was the real murder weapon – not the one in the hidden blue knapsack. But the prosecutors insisted there was only one gun in the shootings, the one in the knapsack.

On September 12th, 2005, two days before the date set for Frances's execution, a Texas newspaper, the *Austin American Statesman*, claimed: "The public cannot be certain of her guilt, but she's going to die for the crime anyway. She was denied a basic requirement for a fair trial – a competent lawyer."

Gloria Rubac, an opponent of the death penalty and

co-founder of a "Free Frances" website, declared: "We're calling for a stay of execution because there are so many unanswered questions in this case. We're also calling for a stay because she had one of the worst lawyers that Harris County has appointed. He has sent 16 people to Death Row – Frances is one of four who are still alive.

"And we're calling for a stay because just this summer the district attorney admitted on camera that more than one gun was recovered from this crime, a fact they have denied for 18 years.

"Given the lack of representation and the prosecutorial misconduct, you can't execute people when there are these doubts. On top of all this, the Houston police crime lab, which has been discredited, was responsible for processing evidence in France's case."

On Death Row Frances Newton was sanguine. "It is difficult being away from my family," she said. "I have always kind of been with all of my brothers and sisters. I have always been kind of insulated, you know, and always had my family around me. So it's been kind of hard not having that, and then under the cloud of guilt that I am, losing my husband and children.

"That's been difficult, but I just take it one day at a time. I cope, with the support I have, the love from my family and friends, the love that I have for my husband and children, and just knowing my own innocence – that helps a lot. I cope, knowing that I have people fighting for me who are believing in me, and believing that the right thing will be done."

Listening to her, Congresswoman Sheila Jackson Lee said she couldn't think of her as anything but a sister, and a mother who had lost her children. The catastrophe of Hurricane Katrina, she said rather theatrically, equalled "the catastrophe of injustice that would occur if Frances goes to her death."

She was working with two congressmen, she said, to try to reach the state governor, Rick Perry, and to contact the solicitor-general to petition the United States Supreme Court for a stay of execution. She would be asking the governor to recognise, as the American Bar Association had done, that justice had not been served.

More than one weapon was now said to have been found, she went on. And there was the matter of right of trial with effective defence counsel.

"Frances Newton received none of that. It is clear that if you have counsel who did not investigate or ask one question of a single witness and posed no defence, you did not have an effective trial.

"A simple act can answer the question, a simple fair act. Not one that says today we release Frances Newton, today we set her free. It is simply to say that what the court system, what the case law, what the Constitution demands, is for the justice system not to send Frances Newton to her death on a lie, but to allow the new evidence to be presented to a jury of her peers."

Another lie, the congresswoman added, was the suggestion that Frances had orchestrated the insurance policies. "We have come to understand that the insurance was sold to her. She did not ask for it. There is no evidence that she killed to gain from the insurance proceeds. This is just one of the lies that have constantly plagued this case."

But the last-minute legal and political bids to save Frances all failed. On September 14th, 2005, her parents were among the witnesses who watched as she was strapped to the death chamber trolley. She declined to make a final statement, saying "No," and shaking her head when the warden asked if she wished to say anything.

She was now 40, and about to become the first black woman to be put to death in Texas since before the American Civil War, and the third woman to be dispatched in that state since executions resumed in 1982 after a moratorium.

She turned her head briefly to look at her family as the lethal injection's drugs began flowing. She seemed to try to mouth something to her relatives, but the drugs kicked in. She coughed once and gasped as her eyes closed. Eight minutes later she was pronounced dead.

One of her sisters buried her head in her arms. Her parents held hands and wiped away a tear, before they walked to the back of the death chamber to comfort their other daughter.

Outside, about 50 demonstrators chanted – a small number compared with the hundreds who assembled in 1998 to protest against the execution of Karla Faye Tucker, the first woman to be put to death in Texas since the Civil War.

Two of Adrian Newton's cousins were also among those who watched Frances Newton die. They complained that too much attention had been focused on the convicted killer and not enough on her three victims. One of them, Tamika Craft-Deeming, sobbed loudly in the death chamber. "I'd like to say not one tear was for Frances," she told reporters after the execution. "They were for the kids."

•

Attorney Ron Mock is not the only lawyer who has been accused of falling asleep during a trial. In 1984 Joe Cannon dozed off up to 10 times for as long as 10 minutes at a time during Calvin Burdine's trial in Texas.

Burdine was found guilty of murdering his gay lover and sentenced to death in 1984, but in August, 2001, a US appeals court ruled that he should have a new trial because his lawyer fell asleep.

In 1987 he came within minutes of being executed before a court ordered a reprieve. Then in October, 2000, a court ruled that although Mr. Cannon fell asleep during the 1984 trial it had not been during the important parts of the trial, and therefore the murder conviction and death sentence were upheld.

Burdine's new lawyer, Robert McGlasson, welcomed the third appeal in 2001. "Finally, common sense has prevailed," he said. "The full court has affirmed what we have said all along, namely that a sleeping attorney is the same as no attorney, and that a death penalty trial conducted under these circumstances violates basic notions of fairness and decency."

Burdine's case generated a lot of publicity. But one aspect has surprisingly attracted little comment. During his closing arguments at the original trial, the prosecutor said "sending a homosexual to the penitentiary certainly isn't a very bad punishment for a homosexual." Where many defence lawyers would have objected. Mr. Cannon let this pass without comment.

Perhaps he was asleep at the time.

WOMEN EXECUTED IN AMERICA
1900–2005

Date of execution	Name	Race	State	Method
17th July 1903	Dora Wright	Black	Oklahoma	Hanging
8th December 1905	Mary Rogers	White	Vermont	Hanging
29th March 1909	Mary Farmer	White	New York	Electrocution
16th August 1912	Virginia Christian	Black	Virginia	Electrocution
13th January 1922	Pattie Perdue	Black	Missouri	Hanging
12th January 1928	Ruth Snyder	White	New York	Electrocution
1st February 1929	Ada Leboeuf	White	Louisiana	Hanging
24th January 1930	Silena Gilmore	Black	Alabama	Electrocution
21st February 1930	Eva Dugan	White	Arizona	Hanging
23rd February 1931	Irene Schroeder	White	Pennsylvania	Electrocution
9th August 1934	Anna Antonio	White	New York	Electrocution
8th February 1935	Julia Moore	Oriental	Louisiana	Hanging
7th June 1935	May Carey	White	Delaware	Hanging
27th June 1935	Eva Coo	White	New York	Electrocution
16th July 1936	Mary Creighton	White	New York	Electrocution
29th April 1937	Mary Holmes	Black	Mississippi	Hanging
28th January 1938	Marie Porter	White	Illinois	Electrocution

Date of execution	Name	Race	State	Method
7th December 1938	Anna Hahn	White	Ohio	Electrocution
21st November 1941	Juanita Spinelli	White	California	Gas chamber
28th November 1942	Toni Henry	White	Louisiana	Electrocution
1st January 1943	Rosanna Phillips	Black	N. Carolina	Gas chamber
15th January 1943	Sue Logue	White	S. Carolina	Electrocution
19th May 1944	Mildred Johnson	Black	Mississippi	Electrocution
16th November 1944	Helen Fowler	Black	New York	Electrocution
29th December 1944	Bessie Williams	Black	N. Carolina	Gas chamber
5th March 1945	Lena Baker	Black	Georgia	Electrocution
7th January 1946	Shellie McKeithen	Oriental	Pennsylvania	Electrocution
14th October 1946	Corrine Sikes	Black	Pennsylvania	Electrocution
17th January 1947	Rosa Stinette	Black	S. Carolina	Electrocution
11th April 1947	Louise Peete	White	California	Gas chamber
7th March 1951	Martha Beck	White	New York	Electrocution
19th June 1953	Ethel Rosenberg	White	New York	Electrocution
4th September 1953	Earle Dennison	White	Alabama	Electrocution
18th December 1953	Bonnie Heady	White	Missouri	Gas chamber
15th January 1954	Dovie Dean	White	Ohio	Electrocution
12th June 1954	Betty Butler	Black	Ohio	Electrocution

Women Executed In America 1900–2005

Date of execution	Name	Race	State	Method
3rd June 1955	Barbara Graham	White	California	Gas chamber
11th October 1957	Rhonda Martin	White	Alabama	Electrocution
8th August 1962	Elizabeth Duncan	White	California	Gas chamber
2nd November 1984	Velma Barfield	White	N. Carolina	Lethal injection
3rd February 1988	Karla Faye Tucker	White	Texas	Lethal injection
30th March 1998	Judy Buenoano	White	Florida	Electrocution
24th February 2000	Betty Lou Beets	White	Texas	Lethal injection
2nd May 2000	Christina Riggs	White	Arkansas	Lethal injection
11th January 2001	Wanda Jean Allen	Black	Oklahoma	Lethal injection
1st May 2001	Marilyn Plantz	White	Oklahoma	Lethal injection
4th December 2001	Lois Nadean Smith	White	Oklahoma	Lethal injection
10th May 2002	Lynda Lyon Block	White	Alabama	Electrocution
8th October 2002	Aileen Wuornos	White	Florida	Lethal injection
14th September 2005	Frances Newton	Black	Texas	Lethal injection

PART TWO

WHAT MAKES A WOMAN KILL?

A case history analysis of some of the attitudes and events that turn the tender sex into homicidal machines

Some women will go so far for love that they will kill for it. Take Karla Homolka, a stunning blonde who was 17 and living in St. Catherine's, Ontario, when she met Paul Bernardo, 23, a student accountant, in 1989. For her it was love at first sight – she fell head over heels for him.

She was so much in love with Bernardo that he could do nothing wrong in her eyes. She complied with all his bizarre sexual whims without question. Unable to satisfy his voracious sexual appetite, she began helping him to find young girls for sex. Even when he killed two teenagers after torturing them, as far as she was concerned he was doing nothing wrong.

Why? The answer is that deep down she was also convinced that unless she did all he wanted, she would lose him. Fear that their lover might just get up and walk away forever haunts many women who are blinded by love.

In Karla's case there was an added complication. She knew he fancied her young sister Tammy, whose clothes she sometimes had to wear to please him. One day when all three were watching a video at her home Karla popped an animal tranquilliser into her sister's drink. As Tammy lost consciousness Bernardo and Karla both had sex with her, videotaping each other's performance.

Then Tammy vomited. They called paramedics, who took her to hospital, where she died the next day. Karla and her boy friend said nothing about the tranquilliser and the inquest coroner decided that Tammy had choked on her own vomit.

When the couple married Karla was unaware that

Bernardo was the local serial rapist being sought by the police. The romance of their Hawaii honeymoon was still lingering in the air when, on the afternoon of April 16th, 1992, they abducted 16-year-old Kristin French as she was walking home from school in St. Catherine's.

Witnesses said that the woman in the car, identified as Karla, opened the door to ask directions, then the woman's male companion, Bernardo, snatched the girl, hauling her into the vehicle.

They imprisoned Kristin in a soundproof room and subjected her to 13 days of videotaped sexual assaults, while showing her videotapes of another girl who Bernardo had murdered and cut up with a chainsaw. Some time later, Kristin's naked corpse was found in a ditch near where another Bernardo victim's body was discovered.

The murderous partnership came to an end in January 1993 when Bernardo gave his wife a severe thrashing with a torch, nearly knocking one of her eyes out of its socket. She was taken to hospital and the police were called. Her subsequent story led to Bernardo's arrest.

Karla was unquestioningly married to a psychopath, but was it only love that blinded her to his horrific behaviour and compelled her to participate in it? Not quite, if some of her friends are to be believed. They described her as "aggressive, pushy, and non-conformist."

After she and her husband were arrested it emerged that she had sexually assaulted and drugged one young girl when her husband wasn't even present. She videotaped the performance and, according to those who saw the tape, she enjoyed it.

The couple were tried separately. Karla was sentenced to 12 years and at Bernardo's trial in 1995 her testimony against him resulted in him being jailed for life.

•

To recognise why some women kill you don't have to look much farther than the seven deadly sins. Jealousy, the most pervasive, perhaps, lurks in the darkest corners of the mind, and can be the inspiration for dreadful deeds. Hell hath no fury like a woman scorned – particularly if the reason for it happens to be another woman.

In Britain, obsessive jealousy drove Rena Salmon to kill after her husband had an affair with her married friend and neighbour, Lorna Rodriguez.

The two couples lived in Hungerford, in Berkshire. Lorna had a successful beauty parlour in west London, so her husband agreed to become a house-husband, staying at home looking after the children while Lorna went to work every day.

Paul Salmon began his affair with Lorna Rodriguez in 2001. They fell madly in love and the following year he and Lorna moved into a house together. When the jilted wife Rena heard they were hoping to have a child she was devastated. She threatened and assaulted the lovers, and made two suicide attempts.

There was, however, much more to all this than sexual rivalry. More than most, perhaps, this really is a case where the killer's background deserves study and sympathy, because the apparent provocation Rena suffered went far beyond the act of adultery.

Rena was the daughter of a white prostitute and her Asian client, and was dark-skinned. When she was a child her mother had angrily imbued her with the idea that she would have preferred a pure white daughter, and regularly scrubbed her with bleach while reminding her that she was paid 10 shillings for the rendezvous with the Asian that resulted in her giving birth.

The effect of this on Rena's self-esteem was understandably catastrophic. But as she grew up, built a life for herself and married Paul, who had an £80,000-a-year information technology job, she felt entitled to hold up her head and say to herself that her horrific childhood could now be forgotten.

Then Lorna, who had gone off with her husband Paul, told her: "We're hoping to have a child and that it will be like us." For Rena, the irresistible inference of this message was that it would be white.

According to Rena, her husband blamed her for being

unable to see Lorna. Rena told him: "If that's how you feel, there's not much point in me being here. There's not much point in me being alive."

She was later to say: "I went to Lorna's and banged on the door at the back. She came out smiling and said, 'You are fat, you are ugly, and you are boring.' So I smacked her one. She hit me back and we started fighting."

A few days later her husband phoned her from a hotel where he was staying with Lorna. Rena said: "I told him not to take Lorna anywhere near our second home in Dorset because I would be there that weekend with the kids. He rang back and said, 'I can shag Lorna just as easily in your bed as I can in the one in Dorset.'"

At 10.30 a.m. on September 10th, 2002, Rena strode down Chiswick High Road, London, towards Lorna's beauty parlour, carrying a double-barrelled shotgun under her arm. She went into the shop and down the stairs to where Lorna was working.

"Hello, Rena," Lorna said, looking up. "Have you come to shoot me?"

"Yes," Rena replied.

There followed what witnesses described as "a very controlled conversation about the future of their children." Then, pointing the gun at Lorna, Rena fired. As Lorna crumpled on the floor, Rena fired again.

Rena was later to say that after phoning for an ambulance she held her dying rival's hand, and, "Lorna squeezed my hand in return."

When she was arrested she referred to her husband, crying, "He will never forgive me now! He will never forgive me now!" The verdict at her trial was a foregone conclusion and she was jailed for life.

•

Women who are deeply in love sometimes express their feelings through the external violence of their emotions. When this happens it seems to their partner that the only way they can express their feelings is by screaming and shouting, like a kettle that shows it is boiling by blowing its top.

The woman wants to fight, argue, hit out, and when all the emotion is released she wants to come together with her partner in a blaze of unbridled lovemaking. It's hard to live with someone like that, as Lee Harvey found out tragically to his cost.

At the height of a terrific row between them, his fiancée Tracie Andrews stabbed him frenetically 30 times. He tried to move away but she had already severed his carotid artery and his jugular vein, causing a massive spurting of blood from his neck. He could not have moved far before collapsing on the ground and dying.

Tracie Andrews had a reputation for expressing her feelings extrovertly and violently for the entire world to hear. At her trial witnesses spoke of violent rows between the couple. A barmaid said she had once tended a cut in Mr. Harvey's neck. She described the wound as resembling "a bite into an apple," and said he also had deep scratches on his cheek.

Another witness said he had once been standing 15 feet away from the couple in a nightclub and saw Tracie beat and punch her boy friend.

A neighbour told of hearing frequent rows between the couple, who were living in the flat below her. The rows had been going on for at least six months, two, three, or more times a week, lasting for hours at a time and sometimes for days. The witness said she often turned up the volume on her TV so that she couldn't hear Lee Harvey calling Tracie a slag and a slut, while Tracie called him a bastard.

When the couple argued Lee would sometimes move out of the flat and return to his parents' home until things cooled down. Then he would go back to the flat – until the next time.

On one occasion the police were called to the flat, where they found Tracie standing amid broken electronic equipment. She complained that Lee had thrown a portable TV and video at her. The two officers gave advice and left.

Most people could not reconcile this kind of behaviour with love. But the truth is that with others it works; for them, it is love. Notice that Lee Harvey always went back, that they were always reconciled, for a short time at least.

Possibly such behaviour is rooted in insecurity, possibly by a deep desire to express, even in a contrary way, feelings that cannot be expressed normally because of emotional repression. The danger of course is that it becomes so violent that it leads to bodily harm or even, as in this case, murder.

Love can surely be the only reason for which Tracie Andrews murdered Lee Harvey. They both had had previous long-term relationships with another person, so they could scarcely be described as immature.

On the fatal night, December 1st, 1996, they had been at a pub together and were driving home when they started arguing. Lee Harvey stopped the car and the fatal stabbing took place, "a most vicious attack," according to the prosecutor at Tracie's trial. To cover her guilt, she concocted a nonsensical story about a road rage driver who had attacked her boy friend before driving off. There was no other driver, and the court rejected the story.

The state of Tracie's mind began to reveal itself after her arrest. Yes, she told detectives, they often argued, but they were deeply in love. They had split up six times, "but we always get back together."

They were a glamorous couple – he tall and handsome, she with her model looks. She didn't really have a motive for murder as much as a motive for marriage. When she gave evidence at her trial she was frank about her relationship with Harvey.

"It was very, very loving and stormy at times," she told the jury. She had attempted suicide after Harvey's death. "I loved him more than anything in the world, and I believe he loved me."

Notice how many times the word love appears in her testimony. She might have done better to plead the exigencies of love, rather than a piece of road rage fiction, as her defence. But perhaps not, for in a sombre court of law such an abstract emotion is not easily understood.

She was asked, for instance: "It must require a real intensity of feeling to put your teeth into someone's neck. It's no mild emotion, is it?"

She replied: "People do things. Lee has done things to me."

Found guilty on July 29th, 1997, Tracie Andrews was sent to jail for life.

•

Tracie was driven by passion, and passion also ruled the waves in the tempestuous life of the unrelated Jane Andrews. The clues to Jane's irrational, theatrical character were best provided by her boy friends, many of whom had stories of the hard times she had given them. One told how when their relationship began to break up, she assaulted him, stalked him, made threatening phone calls, vandalised his car, and fraudulently cashed one of his cheques.

She phoned another ex-lover saying she was in an abortion clinic and her child would die if he didn't return to her. Then, having got him to pay for her fictitious abortion, she ransacked his flat.

Other men who briefly knew her likened her carryings-on to the psychotic behaviour of the spurned lover in the film *Fatal Attraction*.

The fate of Thomas Cressman, 39, the last man in Jane's life, was far more tragic. She murdered him.

Jane had achieved some minor celebrity status when for a time she was the Duchess of York's dresser and personal assistant. She was made redundant in a cost-cutting exercise, but she was still in touch with the duchess when she began a 16-month romantic affair with Cressman.

Things began to go badly downhill when she realised that the affair was not going to last, and her hopes of marriage to him were evaporating. Madly possessive and desperate for a long-term relationship, she threatened suicide to get the attention she needed. But as hope died, anger rose up in her, and with it a deep desire for revenge.

The murder of Thomas Cressman was much more premeditated than Jane Andrews was prepared to admit. While not planned long in advance, it was no sudden attack either. There was plenty of time for common sense to put a brake on her emotions, but the obsessive passion that had taken possession of her would not be sloughed off that quickly.

Their relationship had become extremely fragile when they went on holiday to Cannes in the summer of 2000. When the holiday was over they drove to Nice airport with two of Cressman's relatives in the back of the car. The atmosphere during the journey was very tense.

Later, at Jane's trial, the prosecutor was to say that her way of dealing with this situation "was to get on her mobile phone to her various friends and speak about their relationship, saying that Thomas Cressman had been unpleasant to her, would not marry her, and that she had wasted two years of her life."

At Nice airport they had a blazing row, apparently over Cressman's interest in another woman. Friends said he arrived home "with a face like thunder."

"Her displeasure at his disinclination to marry continued after they got back to London. Things became so difficult that Cressman phoned the police, saying, 'We're rowing. Someone is going to get hurt unless...I would like the police to come and split us up. I would like someone to come round to stop us hurting each other.'"

The police, however, would not intervene before an offence was committed.

That night Cressman was in bed when Jane Andrews first disabled him by striking him with a cricket bat, then went downstairs, fetched a knife, and stabbed him repeatedly. She spent some time washing blood off items before driving to Plymouth. When the murder was discovered and the hunt for her began, she used her mobile phone to call friends pretending she knew nothing of the attack and was unaware that Cressman was dead.

She sent a text to a friend: "I have just heard on the radio that Tommy has been murdered. I cannot believe it. I am dying inside. My heart is broken."

It was erratic and unrealistic behaviour, and from all accounts typical of her. As her ex-husband testified at her trial, she was "prone to melodrama" when upset. Cressman clearly suffered from this melodrama, for in his last letter to her he wrote: "Your mood swings have been so hard to predict." Jane Andrews herself told the police that her Cannes holiday had ended in friction when she again raised the question of marriage and kept pressing for an answer. But a friend said: "Tommy felt she was too unstable. Was this sort of thing, he wondered, going to occur every time they had a disagreement?"

Instability, mood swings, melodrama – these are all hallmarks of women driven by intense passion, when normality goes out of the window and is replaced by behaviour for which there can be no rationale. "You killed the man you loved and ruined your own life," the judge told her, sentencing her to life. "You made your attack on him when you were consumed with anger and bitterness."

•

Uncontrollable anger fuelled by uncontrollable passion was the driving force behind the senseless murder committed by Heather Stephenson-Snell. Although her own mind was a welter of grim fantasies, she founded a psychotherapy clinic in York to help people with mind problems.

Despite her cut-glass name and veneer of respectability, Heather saw herself as wild and unconventional. She turned her clinic into a fortress, protected by six-foot gates, Rottweilers and razor wire. She also set up an all-female chapter of the Hell's Angels.

When she learned that her boy friend John Williams had left her and moved in with a mother of two – who we shall call Mrs. June Day – she went berserk. For 19 months she stalked the couple in disguise and, under cover of night, bombarded June Day with threatening and indecent calls.

On the night of Halloween, 2002, she set out to murder Mrs. Day, laying her plans in such a way that suspicion would fall on John Williams. Donning a *Scream* mask and armed with a shotgun, she drove to the couple's home and banged on their door. It was then past midnight, and the noise she made so irritated neighbour Bob Wilkie that he came out to remonstrate with her.

The well-laid murder plan was thrust aside when Heather swivelled round, pulled the shotgun from under her cloak and fired point-blank at the irritated neighbour. Bob Wilkie died as he fell.

Psychiatric reports read at her subsequent trial for murder revealed a personality that bore an uncanny resemblance to that of Jane Andrews. The reports confirmed what everyone in the courtroom had already discovered – that she had a histrionic personality disorder and loved nothing more than to create a drama that made her the centre of attention.

Heather Stephenson-Snell, then aged 47, was sentenced to life, the judge ordering that she serve at least 22 years.

•

The inevitable man was present most of the time when Carol Bundy became a murderer, but she definitely got her own sexual kicks out of killing. In the summer of 1980 she went on a killing spree with boy friend Douglas Clark, who was eventually charged with six murders. He said he had killed perhaps 50 people in total and was hoping to kill 100 in pursuit of "kinky sex."

During the spree Carol, a plump, 37-year-old nurse, killed and beheaded former boy friend Jack Murray. Beheading their victims was a favourite pastime of this double act. Carol told police that Clark once took home the head of a prostitute he had decapitated after shooting her while she was giving him oral sex.

He froze the head in the freezer, after which Carol would paint the face with make-up "like a Barbie doll" so that Clark could have sex with it again. Clark would swing the head around by the hair and take it into the shower with him, where he would orally copulate with it. According to Carol, "he thought it was as funny as hell." Eventually they discarded the head in the driveway of a house.

Carol's assertion that she participated in these acts because she was in thrall to Clark had a hollow ring to it when she added: "The broad was dead anyway. What was the harm in it?"

She would accompany Clark on trips to find prostitutes and kill them after he had oral sex with them. She thought of herself, she said, as Clark's slave – "I felt I had no alternative but to join in with him." When she was upset and talked about committing suicide, Clark told her: "I would like you to hang yourself up, so that I can have intercourse with you as you die." She didn't seem to demur at the idea, although she didn't commit suicide.

She undoubtedly imagined that all her co-operation in the killings would make Clark love her more. The reverse seemed to happen. Eventually he would sleep with her only in a *ménage à trois* with an 11-year-old girl, with whom they both had oral sex.

It was at this point that she killed and decapitated Jack Murray. The decapitation was held to be a final desperate act to gain Clark's approval, knowing how fond he was of cutting off victims' heads. That didn't work, either, so she went to the police.

Carol Bundy watched her lover kill young girls and took part in at least one of the murders. She killed her former lover and cut off his head. She painted a decapitated head so that her lover could have oral sex with it. She knew that all this heightened her lover's sex drive – and although a mountain of blame for her acts has been laid off on her boy friend, all the evidence suggest that she got sexual kicks from killing.

The couple were tried separately. Clark was given six
death sentences, one for each of the six murders for which
he was charged. As each sentence was read out separately
he snapped at the judge: "Smile when you say that!" Carol
Bundy received a 52-year sentence. On December 9th,
2003, she died of a heart attack. She was 61.

•

At 28 Maria Hnatiuk, daughter of a Ukrainian father and
a German mother, was a woman of the world, sexually
experienced and with a voracious erotic appetite. She
made love to men and women alike – the sexual urge for
her was a permanent, insatiable itch.

Like Carol Bundy, Maria claimed she was enslaved to
a boy friend, who she met while working in Norwich.
She said she allowed him to take over and change her
completely. He made her wear dowdy clothes, PVC
fetish outfits and dog collars. He bullied her into bringing
women home so that he could watch lesbian sex sessions
before joining in.

One woman, 18-year-old Rachel Lean, became a close
friend after they met in July, 1995, but when the women
went for a stroll together Maria suddenly produced a
knife and stabbed Rachel 57 times. She hid the body in
a nearby copse, where it lay undiscovered for five days.
When it was found police felt it was significant that
Rachel's leggings had been pulled down to expose her
buttocks.

Arrested, Maria made a statement redolent of Carol
Bundy. Refusing to accept full blame for the murder,
she claimed that her boy friend had reduced her to a
mental state in which she had to kill Rachel in order to
keep him.

At her trial, when she was sentenced to life for Rachel's
murder, the prosecution produced two witnesses who
testified that Maria had enjoyed sexual threesomes with
them for many years.

•

We should not forget greed as a motivation for murder, in women just as much as in men.

The glint of a golden reward is attractive to an unhappy wife – sometimes even to a happy one. There is no deep psychological reason for it – greed simply exists more in some people than in others. It existed very strongly in Deborah Winzar.

A qualified nurse, she married, in 1985, Dominic McCarthy, who the previous year was paralysed in a road accident and confined to a wheelchair for life. Five years after their marriage he was awarded £600,000 compensation.

That was the sort of money Deborah couldn't resist. At the end of January, 1997, she injected her husband with a massive dose of insulin and then went to a party. McCarthy was found the next morning lying on his bed in a coma, having inhaled vomit.

He was rushed to hospital, where his life support equipment failed twice – both times after a visit from his wife. On February 9th, 1997, he died without emerging from his coma. The investigation that followed was long and difficult, but it resulted in Deborah Winzar's trial for murder on June 8th, 2000.

The motive suggested by the prosecution was the value of the house they jointly owned in Stonely, Cambridgeshire, and the £415,000 she stood to collect in investments. Without her husband's knowledge, she had switched six of his investments into her own name.

The irony of it all was that although his wife gave him a huge insulin dose, it wasn't quite enough to kill him at once. Although he was only 34, Dominic McCarthy was grossly overweight, and the sudden death at home of the 20-stone paraplegic would not have been considered suspicious had it not been for the blood tests routinely taken when he was rushed to hospital. It was these blood tests that revealed the presence of insulin.

Deborah Winzar was sentenced to life imprisonment,

giving her plenty of time to mull over her terrible greed.

•

Deborah made her play for her husband's money a few years after they were married, but Mrs. Jean Daddow, of Northiam, East Sussex, actually planned to kill her husband Terry for his cash even before she married him.

Terry Daddow wasn't above reproach. He was thought to have swindled half a million pounds out of vulnerable old people as a financial adviser. This was the money his wife wanted. For her he represented a victim worth at least £300,000 – but only if he were dead.

For months she slipped LSD into his food to give him hallucinations and to increase the depression to which he was prone. Then she hired hit-man Robert Bell to kill Daddow for a fee of £7,000. After a number of bungled attempts Bell blasted the unwanted husband with a shotgun on his own doorstep.

On May 19th, 1993, Bell was jailed for life. Jean Daddow and Roger Blackman, Bell's accomplice, were both jailed for 18 years for conspiracy to murder. After the trial a detective described Jean Daddow as "one of the most evil women I have ever known. She was driven by a lust for money. It may be that she married Terry Daddow just to kill him."

•

Only hours after Dena Thompson killed Julian Webb, a man she married bigamously, she went to his employers to ask for his £35,000 death benefit. She had tricked Webb into taking large quantities of lethal drugs when he had no idea that what he was swallowing might kill him. In December, 2003, she was jailed for life for his murder.

For Dena Thompson, killing a bigamous husband was all in a day's work. In her career as a con-woman she was said to have netted around £500,000, by spinning hard luck stories to men to part them from their savings. She prompted a detective to remark: "She is every man's nightmare. For a decade she has targeted men sexually, financially and physically. I am very glad to see her behind bars."

•

Few people understood exactly why Jane Toppan had a killing nature. She murdered, by her own call, more than 100 people, and each time she described symptoms that equated with a sexual climax. She sought love so that she could eject it; kindness so that she could spurn it, and sexual delight in killing. Her psyche was completely inside out.

Jane was pink, plump and motherly – the kind of woman you used to see in advertisements for "home-made" pies and jams. But at her trial in Lowell, Massachusetts, in the summer of 1902, she confessed that she wanted to be known as the greatest criminal who ever lived.

"That is my ambition," she told a court of horrified spectators, "to kill more people – more helpless people – than any man or woman has ever killed."

She was 38, and had once had the reputation among Lowell doctors of being the community's finest and most capable nurse. It turned out she had been all too capable – she had turned more than a hundred sick beds into death beds. That is probably how many she had poisoned with her own strange mixture of morphine, atropine and whisky.

Jane's behaviour all her life was in inverse ratio to the norm. The more people were kind to her, the more she hated them. Hers was a private war against kindness and her own personal obscurity. All her victims were people who had shown some affection towards her.

A talented amateur chemist, she devised a poison that left scarcely a trace in her patient's bloodstream after death, but which, when administered bit by bit over a period of some days, guaranteed a lingering and painful death.

This was the sad and frightening story of a girl who needed desperately to prove to herself and to the world that she was of some importance, and not simply a poor and unwanted orphan. The world would sit up and take notice of Jane Toppan – she would see to that. She would get her own back on a society that had cast her aside as trash.

Her family tree was a twisted one. Her mother committed suicide, stabbing herself with a pair of scissors, in her husband's tailoring shop, when Jane was only two years old. Jane was the youngest of four daughters and the quietest of the four when, a year later, her father was committed to an insane asylum.

She and her sisters were sent to a Boston orphanage. Her eldest sister, Mary, was an imbecile, and died early. Louisa, the blonde beauty of the family, became a prostitute, plying Boston's city streets for clients. The third sister, Mae, married a wealthy Chicago cattleman – proving to be the white sheep of the family.

When Jane was five, she was adopted by Abner Toppan and his family, of Lowell. They gave the lonely and bewildered little girl everything, including their family name.

She was a dark-eyed child. She laughed and smiled constantly – but behind the laughter was an agony and fright such as only a child can know. Comfort, love and security – all of these had come too late. Yet she was only five.

"Whenever she was particularly pleased about anything, she would laugh and clap her hands," Abner Toppan said later. "But even when she was naughty and we had to punish her – even then she smiled. We didn't understand her."

Who would? Throughout her entire life, Jane punished those who had shown her sympathy and kindness. When her stepsister Edith Toppan, 10 years her senior, took Jane under her wing and guided her into a career as a nurse, Edith was signing her own death warrant. In 1899 Edith fell ill with a bad cold and fever.

There was no question about it – she must have Jane

to nurse her back to health. Soon after Jane arrived on the scene, the bad cold had developed into pneumonia. Even so, Edith's doctor was only too pleased to have the services of such a dedicated and efficient nurse.

Jane had a precise ritual of killing. She would first build up her patient to the point where the attending doctor was encouraged. Then, after the doctor stopped making regular calls, she would begin the ceremony. She would sit at the bedside table with two vials in her hands, one containing morphine, the other, atropine. Atropine is a poisonous white crystalline alkaloid extracted from belladonna and has the effect of enlarging the pupils of the eyes.

First, she would administer the morphine which in due time would reduce the pupils to pinpoints. Then the atropine was given, and slowly the pupils would dilate. Both drugs were administered in a solution of whisky, which helped to erase the signs of poisoning.

She would alternate the two drugs, increasing the dosage day by day. The patient's breath would become short and painful. Then their body would be seized with convulsions, then become lax, then chill, and then again the convulsions. As the climax approached and the patient neared death, Jane would become increasingly excited.

"I can't quite describe the sensation," she said at her trial. "I wanted to laugh. I would kiss the patient – simply because I was happy. I remember kissing Edith. She still thought I was trying to save her. If it hadn't been for her I would never have been a nurse – and now I was paying her back."

"Paying her back, Miss Toppan?" Her own lawyer was bewildered by his client's remark. "What do you mean by paying her back?"

Jane replied: "I don't know. She had been very kind to me."

The court listened in silence as the story of her training as a nurse was revealed. "Her interest in the chemistry of medicines was extraordinary," one of her instructors reported. "She knew more about the composition of drugs than any doctor in the state by the time she was fully trained."

"Yes, I knew even then what I wanted to do," she said enthusiastically. "I knew I would be on trial some day – and I was only 16!"

When she was 18 she met the only man in her life. He was Charlie May, who worked in a bookshop. They read love stories together, but he drifted away and married another woman, probably saving his own life in the process. Or was he the catalyst that set her on her career of killing?

"It was shortly after Charlie went that I first killed one of my patients," she said. "I was just experimenting, really. I always keep a dream book. The day on which I started the experiment my book said: 'Good day. Dreams soon to be realised.' I still have the same book. I underlined that day. It was May 17th, 1883, but the patient didn't die until several days later."

How many deaths she was actually responsible for in the 18 years between 1883 and 1901, when she was finally arrested, she wasn't quite sure. "In the beginning I was a novice. And of course I didn't kill everyone. I was a very fine nurse and every doctor in Lowell will tell you so.

"It was only the patients who were particularly kind to me, the ones I liked, that I poisoned. At first I couldn't tell whether they might have died by natural causes. But there were at least a hundred I did kill."

Thirty-one deaths were verified by the state – that many bodies were exhumed. In other instances, relatives of the deceased refused to permit exhumation – Jane had enough blood to her credit.

Besides being a killer, she was an arsonist. If she were at all uncertain as to how many lives she had taken, she was perfectly certain about the number of houses she had burned down. There were eight of them. "All of them belonged to people who had befriended me. I had killed two daughters in one of the houses and the father in another one. But in the other six, I hurt no one, except, of course, that I burned down their homes."

One of her patients was Ellery Sedgwick, who later became the editor of *The Atlantic Monthly* and a distinguished writer. Sedgwick became seriously ill with pneumonia while studying at Harvard. By that time Jane was well into her homicidal career, but for some reason she decided against giving the young undergraduate the Toppan treatment, possibly because he reminded her of her romance with Charlie May.

In any event, Sedgwick, who became something of a friend to his nurse in later life, rewarded Jane by writing one of his most famous essays about her. That was just what she was after – a strange glory, a horrible fame. In his essay Sedgwick said: "When it comes to evaluating the histories of famous murderers, Jane Toppan has never received proper recognition. Without the slightest doubt, she outranks both Bluebeard and Jack the Ripper."

And still to the people who knew her, she was an excellent New England nurse and a spinster who never missed church, or a church social, and who was as fond of hymn singing as she was of children. But on October 31st, 1901, Hallowe'en day, the roof fell in on this last of the Massachusetts witches, and she was as excited and relieved as anyone. Her day of glory, towards which she had worked for so many years, had finally arrived. She was arrested.

The patient responsible for it was Mrs. Alden Davies. She had been Jane's patient several years ago. Under Jane's care she had recovered from a near-fatal illness, and while she had no particular regard for her nurse at the time of her sickness and convalescence, later she must have reflected: "Jane Toppan is a rare person. She saved my life." And so it was that Mrs. Davies came to adore "our darling Jane," to pay her frequent calls and, in perhaps a little too patronising a manner, began to cultivate her company.

Jane, of course, could put up with anything but kindness, and when Mrs. Davies began to visit her, bringing her little presents of fruit, candy, or books of poetry, then inviting her to tea and dinner, her former nurse must have wished many times that Mrs. Davies would take sick again. But her benefactress seemed as hardy as Plymouth Rock, and either Jane grew desperate or she determined that the hour had come for her to reveal herself.

Mrs. Davies was holidaying at her summer home with her husband and their two married daughters when she decided that the party should be increased to five. "We must have our darling Jane with us," she said one morning. That afternoon she travelled back to Lowell to persuade her one-time nurse to join them.

She was chatting amiably in Jane's sitting-room over a cup of tea when she mentioned that she had been having some bad headaches recently.

"Leave it to me!" exclaimed Jane. She leapt up, and returned a minute later carrying a syringe in which was a deadly mixture of her favourite poisons. Before her visitor had time to react, the nurse pulled up her sleeve and plunged the needle into her arm.

"You'll feel much better in a little while. Your headaches will completely disappear," she said.

She was right about the headaches – they did disappear. Mrs. Davies collapsed and Jane removed her to her own bed. She then sat down and wrote to Mr. Davies informing him that his wife had been taken suddenly ill, but he was not to be alarmed because she would soon be much better in the care of her old nurse.

Two days later Mrs. Davies died. Jane travelled to see her widowed husband and broke the news to his devastated family. Mrs. Davies had a bad heart, she explained, and one might expect her to die without warning.

Mr. Davies was none too strong himself. In fact, news of his wife's death came as such a shock that he took to his own bed. The devoted Jane nursed him there, but her ministrations were to no avail, for 10 days later he too was dead. Sorrowfully his family laid him to rest alongside his wife's body in the local cemetery.

Nurse Jane remembered the funeral well. "They bought so many flowers for him because he was well liked," she said at her trial. "I liked him very much myself. But I wanted to tell his family and all those people who came to the funeral that if they had waited a few days longer I would have saved them a trip to the cemetery, because I had another death waiting for them."

Another death in the family? Was this possible? It was. Four days later, with Jane Toppan still in attendance, Mr. Davies's daughter, Mrs. Mary Gibbs, breathed her last. And three weeks after that, her sister, Mrs. Genevieve Gordon, followed her into the family burial plot.

Mr. Gibbs, husband of Mary Gibbs, scratched his head in bewilderment. Something, he decided, was clearly wrong. He called in the police and insisted they do something. "But Nurse Jane Toppan is above all suspicion," he was told. Mr. Gibbs banged his fist on the table. "Do something!" he shouted. "All these deaths in my family can't be coincidences."

The bodies of the Davies family were secretly exhumed. Post-mortems were performed, but only after checking and double-checking was the evidence of poisoning discovered. At the end there could be no doubt about it – morphine and atropine. And so Jane Toppan was finally brought in for questioning.

On November 9th, 1901, the *New York Tribune* reported from Boston: *"The first positive evidence that Miss Toppan bought drugs or poison was discovered here today when it was learned that last July she attended the Davies family and ordered morphine tablets at Benjamin Waters' drugstore on Main Street.*

"Waters was instructed to send the tablets enclosed in a paper wrapper to Miss Toppan at the Davies home. The druggist says the bottle contained enough poison to kill a score of persons. It was delivered to Miss Toppan and paid for by her, Waters' clerk receiving the money."

On November 15th, 1901, Jane was arraigned before Judge Frederick Swift. A local newspaper reported: "Miss Toppan appeared extremely nervous but, nevertheless, smiled constantly and on one or two occasions, laughed."

Still, she was the dark-eyed and terrified child who smiled while being punished, because punishment was all that Jane understood, and for her it was bound up irrevocably with love.

The trial began in December, but was adjourned until June the following year to allow time for three psychologists to study the case. They, in the end, were frankly bewildered.

"Miss Toppan behaves in a perfectly normal fashion," said one. "Her temper is extremely pleasant. She is well liked by her jailers and by all those who have official contact with her. She reads a great deal when she is alone. She is inclined to be chatty to visitors, speaking of the murders she has committed in a friendly and unemotional fashion."

When asked if she had any pangs of conscience, she replied, "No, none at all, even though some of the patients I poisoned were among the dearest and kindest people I have ever known."

A modern psychoanalyst might not have been so hard put to come up with an explanation for her strange personality. Her earliest memories were of suffering – the unhappiness of her mother, so desperate that she took her own life when Jane was barely able to talk; the torment of her father who, a few years after his wife's death, became hopelessly insane. Jane had never been loved by those from whom love must come. Her parents were involved with their own tragedies, and those tragedies left fearful wounds on their children's souls.

"They called my father Kelly The Crack," she told one of her doctors. "My real name is Kelly, you know. Nora Kelly. That was until I was adopted by the Toppans. I don't know when I first found out that my father was still alive. I was never allowed to see him because he was what we called violent. I don't think I really wanted to see him, anyway. And then later, he died. Actually, I believe I may have been afraid of him."

Instead of love, Jane had been emotionally scarred,

and scarred so deeply that even she knew nothing about it. She could be sweet, motherly and helpful. But put someone like one of her patients utterly in her power, just as she had once been in the power of her parents, and she would use that person as she had been used. Instead of caring for such a person she would try to destroy them, just as she herself had been destroyed.

The fact that she felt impelled to poison the very people who had been most kind to her suggests that she was afraid of kindness and afraid of love. After all, her parents' love had turned into hatred and madness. She would stamp out of her life the possibility that that transformation might occur again. At the same time she would show the world that she could not be overlooked, could not be taken for granted, would not be the neglected child.

"Toppan the Terrible," the newspapers called her during her brief and sensational trial. *"The Angel of Mercy has turned out to be the Angel of Death,"* trumpeted the *New York World* on June 25th, 1902.

Her counsel pleaded insanity, but she laughed merrily at him. "How could I be insane," she said, "if I knew what I was doing? Insane people do not know right from wrong. I knew that what I was doing was wrong, so how could I be insane?"

The entire nation was appalled by what she had to say during those hot June days when she was supposedly pleading for mercy, but actually boasting of her crimes and relishing every headline for which she was responsible. Here is some of her testimony:

"Do you feel no remorse, Miss Toppan, for what you have done?"

"No, I feel just fine."

"When you witnessed a patient's death struggle, didn't your conscience tell you that what you were doing was a monstrous thing?"

"I knew before I started that it was a monstrous thing I was doing. And sometimes I did decide to save the patient. Generally, it was too late. When I was able to save them, it only meant that I would have to do it all over again. Sometimes, though, I waited several weeks before trying again."

As she went on, her mad logic began to fall apart. "The jury is probably right," she said at one point. "Something is very likely wrong with my head. I can't say just what the trouble is. I know that I never felt so well as when I came to and found that one of my patients was dead."

"Exactly what do you mean, Miss Toppan, when you say 'come to'?" her lawyer wanted to know.

She faltered. "I don't know. In the last moments when someone...when they died, I think I loved them most then."

So killing for Jane was a way of making love. She was lost in a destructive ecstasy instead of the creative one she would have known as a normal human being. She would caress the body of her dying patient throughout its torments. At the moment of death, she achieved her greatest joy, a release from consciousness, from the tensions of her life – an experience comparable to that of a sexual climax. She would black out. The victim was dead. Jane returned to earth, but not to the scene of the crime. She felt no guilt.

She was aware of the legal meaning of right and wrong. That is, she knew her acts were punishable by law – but deep inside herself, she didn't know *why* they were. And because she didn't know why, she could legally be called insane.

And that was the jury's verdict.

She was committed for life to a mental institution. She took with her from jail six volumes of Rudyard Kipling, the complete works of Edgar Allen Poe, Louisa May Alcott's *Little Women*, and a scrapbook of her newspaper clippings that she had put together for herself with zealous care.

She smiled as a child when being punished. She smiled when she was imprisoned. She had smiled during her trial. She smiled now as she sat in the asylum, reading, chatting with other patients, turning over the pages of her scrapbook

In her mental hospital, scented with sickness and

sanitation, she fell in love with a book of yellowed newspaper clippings. She was still in love with them when she died in 1938 at the age of 81.

•

Women don't kill nearly as often as men, and the category of victims highest on their killing list is children. That suggests that in the business of murder it is generally the strong that kill the weak. This was the case with Bonnie Heady, an unusually callous woman who killed a child simply out of greed for money.

When Robert Greenlease, a wealthy Missouri car dealer, received a ransom note for the release of his kidnapped son Bobby, he said: "I'll pay. I'll pay any amount I can possibly raise to get my boy back safe and sound."

The ransom demanded, $600,000, was three times as large as any previously recorded in the United States. At the centre of the kidnap was Bonnie Heady, and when she arrived at the main door of six-year-old Bobby Greenlease's school she was breathless and agitated "I've been sent for Bobby," she announced. "I'm his aunt – his mother's sister. It's an emergency."

The school, Kansas City's grandly named French Institute of Notre Dame di Sion, was run by nuns. They asked her to come in, and led her to the sitting-room. Then they asked her to explain further.

"It's Mrs. Greenlease," she said. "We were shopping and she suddenly became ill. It's her heart. She's in St. Mary's Hospital now and I'm afraid her condition is very serious. She asked that Bobby be brought to her at once."

To the nuns, everything about the rather plump woman seemed genuine. She was dressed simply, but tastefully. Her speech and manner were cultured. Outside in the drive, a taxi waited.

"Perhaps you would like to say a prayer for Bobby's mother in our chapel just across the hall, while I bring the boy from his classroom," said the senior nun. Bobby's so-called aunt, the unscrupulous Bonnie Heady, readily agreed. "Yes, I should like to pray. I'm not a Catholic, but maybe God will hear my prayers from your chapel."

More than anything else, this simple manifestation of faith dispelled any lingering doubts in the mind of the senior nun. She fetched the boy and he left with his "aunt," climbing into the waiting taxi. The deception was uncovered only when the acting sister superior, informed of Mrs. Greenlease's heart attack, phoned to inquire about her condition. Mrs. Greenlease herself answered the call, and in a few moments the terrifying truth was all too clear to her. Someone had stolen her son. Hurriedly she called her husband and he phoned the police.

The ruse to snatch the boy from his school showed shrewd planning. Bonnie Heady had played her part to perfection. That morning, September 28th, 1953, the police settled back to wait for the inevitable – a ransom note. Several hours later they intercepted it at the post office.

"Your boy has been kidnapped," it said. *"Get $600,000 in 20s and 10s – fed. res. Notes from all twelve districts. We realise it takes a few days to get that amount. Boy will be in good hands – when you have money ready put ad in K.C. Star – M will meet you in Chicago next Sunday – Mr. G."*

A postscript added: *"$400,000 in 20s, $200,000 in 10s."*

"I'll pay," babbled a distraught Mr. Greenlease. A detective put a kindly hand on his shoulder. There were implicit dangers, he said. Bobby was a bright little boy capable of identifying his abductors, should they be caught after releasing him unharmed. The usual pattern in such cases was to kill the victim of a snatch as a safeguard against any possibility of identification, and then proceed to collect the ransom.

Greenlease nodded. He understood all that, he said. But he wasn't going to be deterred by the risk.

FBI agents arrived to study the ransom note. From an analysis of the technique used by the kidnappers they were convinced they were dealing with criminals of above-average intelligence. The method with which Bobby was taken from his school was daringly simple but efficient.

"And," said an FBI agent, "note the instructions about the money – all tens and twenties, from all federal reserve districts. Even if we recorded the serial numbers on the bills, we'd have some forty thousand widely varying numbers. They could be very hard to spot once they were in circulation."

Haunted by the fear that the kidnappers might already have murdered his son, Mr. Greenlease set the wheels in motion to amass the ransom money. His bank wanted 48 hours to bring all the banknotes together, and assured him of their co-operation.

Meanwhile, a swarm of newspapermen descended on the Greenleases' Mission Hills mansion on the outskirts of Kansas City. A friend of the family treated them to frequent press conferences on the driveway, and dealt briskly with the plethora of crank phone calls and messages, and fake ransom demands. But there was no mistaking the authenticity of the letter that arrived 36 hours after the kidnap. It enclosed a religious medal that Bobby was wearing when he left school with the plump woman – a small Maltese cross on a narrow red ribbon.

During the 48 hours it took to gather the ransom money, the kidnapper phoned frequently. His voice was assured, his speech that of an educated man. "This is M," was his usual introduction. Once he said, "Don't try any tricks, and you'll get the boy back." He would sometimes chat for as long as 10 minutes, apparently indifferent to the risk that a long conversation might enable his calls to be traced.

He was once asked to bring Bobby to the phone. "Maybe next time," he replied. Then on the next call he explained that he couldn't bring the boy to the phone he was speaking from. To the monitoring police, this was understandable. Tracers had pinpointed the calls from phone boxes in the vicinity of a shopping centre.

On the first attempt to deliver the ransom money – dollar bills weighing 85lbs, in 400 bundles, and crammed into an army duffle bag – the instructions were impossible to follow. When the kidnapper called again, the distraught mother grabbed the phone.

"I'm Bobby's mother," Mrs. Greenlease said tensely. "I've got to know he's safe and well. You must prove that to me."

"How, lady?"

"Ask him two questions, then tell me the answers he gives. Ask him the name of the chauffeur we had in Europe last summer. He'll remember the name. And ask him what he was building in his room last Saturday night."

If the abductor had come back with he right answers, this would have proved that Bobby was alive. But when "M" phoned again, he said: "The boy wouldn't answer your questions. He's a sulky brat. Get that money to us and take him off our hands!"

He arranged that the money, still in the duffle bag, should be left in high grass near a country lane. His instructions were obeyed to the letter, but again things didn't go as smoothly as planned. It would later emerge that the kidnapper was drunk, and reeled about in the hedgerow legless. Unable to find the money, he went back to the phone.

On October 4th, 1953, he made his 14th phone call to the Greenleases. A family friend, Robert Ledterman, answered.

"How are you?" the caller asked.

"Fine. How are you tonight?" Ledterman replied.

"A little late, but we're all set. We have a perfect plan," said the kidnapper. "There cannot be any mistake. I want to make sure there's no mix-up this time."

"Yes. Let's get things over. By the way, M, did the boy answer either of those questions?"

"No…I couldn't…we didn't get anything from him."

"Couldn't get anything from him?"

"He wouldn't talk…I'll tell you this much. You will get him in Pittsburg, Kansas. That's the gospel truth."

Following arrangements made during the phone conversation, Ledterman and Norbert O'Neill, another family friend, placed the duffle bag near a bridge at midnight. Some hours later, M called the Greenlease home to report that the kidnappers had collected the ransom but hadn't counted it.

"I can assure you that all the money you asked for is there," Ledterman said.

"Well, I am sure of that. You can tell his mother that she will see him as we promised within twenty-four hours. We will be glad to send him back."

Soon afterwards, a message told Greenlease to go to the telegraph office in Pittsburg, Kansas, and await instructions for the recovery of the boy. The frantic parents hastened to the office, but their long hours of waiting went unrewarded. The instructions never came, and there was no sign of Bobby. The kidnappers had the $600,000, and as far as anyone could tell at that time, they were in the clear.

On the afternoon of October 5th, 1953, as friends of the Greenleases waited in vain at that same telegraph office, another chain of events began.

A cab driver going off duty transferred a fare to a buddy, remarking that the passenger was "a live one with plenty of dough and rarin' to spend it." The cabbies then transferred two heavy suitcases under the watchful eye of the "live one," who said his name was Steve. He was somewhat the worse for drink, but was still managing to stay upright.

With his new driver, Steve started to do the town in the cab, picking up a girl named Ruthie Packer, a willowy blonde, on the way. Then he gave the cabbie $20 and tossed him another $100 "on account." Still later, he handed the astonished driver $2.500, with instructions to return the following morning to the motel where he was staying. The cabbie was to bring along a car, rented in his name, plus a couple of suitcases.

Next morning, Ruthie Packer showed the cab driver $1,000, which she said her friend Steve had given her just to fly to California "to post a letter."

"The guy is nuts," she said. "He's packing a gun, and those two suitcases are packed with dough. I bet he's got a million bucks in them!"

Following Steve's directions, the cabbie now went out and rented him a $185-a-month suite in a St. Louis hotel. As soon as "Steve" had moved in, he sent the cabbie out to find him a girl.

By this time, however, the cabbie had not surprisingly become suspicious of his customer. So instead of getting a girl for Steve, he called the police and told them about the big spender. Within minutes cops surrounded the hotel suite and took "Steve" into custody. They found his suitcases full of money, and a .38 revolver in his pocket.

Shortly after "Steve" was taken to police headquarters, a squad of officers began to count the money. There was $293,992 in tens and twenties.

"We know precisely where those bills came from," Police Chief Dan O'Connell told his prisoner. "You'd better tell us your story."

"Yeah, I might as well," the prisoner replied. "My name is Carl Austin Hall. I'm one of the Kansas City kidnappers."

By the time the Kansas City police chief had arrived in St. Louis by chartered plane, St. Louis detectives had learned a lot about Hall. He was 34, lived in Kansas City, and was on parole from Missouri State Prison, where he had done time for a string of taxi stick-ups. He had a girl friend who, he said, had helped with the kidnapping of Bobby Greenlease, and he took the officers to meet her.

Thus it was that in a flat in Arsenal Street, St. Louis, detectives met Mrs. Bonnie Brown Heady, the plump woman who had so impressed the nuns at Bobby's school, and who was the lover of the rather down-at-heel Carl Hall. A chubby, five-foot-five divorcee from St. Joseph, Missouri, she was fighting a losing battle with a hangover. She was immediately arrested.

For a long time, though, Cal Hall tried to lead the officers along a false trail, claiming that Bobby had been turned over to a third accomplice, who was to have released him when given word that the ransom had been received. If anything had happened to the boy, Hall insisted, this other man was responsible. As for Bonnie Heady, she was an innocent dupe – she hadn't known it was a kidnapping. The FBI swiftly demolished that claim when they matched her fingerprints to those found on the ransom notes.

The true story came out eventually. Even before they kidnapped Bobby, Carl Hall and Bonnie Heady planned to murder the little boy – they had even dug his grave in preparation for it. Bonnie took him from the school to a drugstore car park, where they transferred him to a station wagon. Then they drove him to a wheatfield in Overland Park, a suburb of Kansas City. Hall planned to strangle Bobby there, but the length of rope he had brought along with him was too short. The child struggled and Hall hit him a couple of times before shooting him twice with his .38.

Bonnie Heady stood by and watched the murder take place. After that she helped Hall wrap the body in a plastic sheet. They drove with it to her house in St. Joseph, where they buried the body in the grave they had dug the previous day. They planted chrysanthemums over the grave, and then proceeded to extort the ransom money.

On October 30th, 1953, a federal grand jury indicted Carl Austin Hall and Bonnie Brown Heady for the kidnapping. On November 3rd they pleaded guilty, hoping to escape execution because, under the Lindbergh law, the death penalty could be imposed only on the recommendation of a jury. But Judge Albert Reeves decreed that they must stand trial.

The judge said: "They committed cold-blooded, heartless, first-degree murder. I fail to find any mitigating circumstances in this case."

The jury recommended that the pair should die in the gas chamber, and neither of them appealed They seemed almost to welcome their sentence as a release from a world they didn't seem to want to be part of any more.

Hall was given little time to relax, though, as police

and the FBI grilled him again and again to try to find out what had happened to the missing $300,000 of the ransom money. Discarding the story of the third accomplice, he insisted that, except for what he had spent or given away, all the money had been in the two suitcases and the briefcase found in his hotel suite when he was arrested. Ruthie Packer had long since returned the $1,000 he gave her.

They were assigned to widely separated cells in the basement Death Row at Missouri State Penitentiary in Jefferson City. Special guard details watched them around the clock, and they were allowed no contact with the other prisoners. As an extra precaution, they were fed from the prison officers' mess, and no other prisoners were permitted near their food.

During the one month they spent on Death Row, neither took any exercise in the prison yard – in fact, neither displayed much energy. They lay on their bunks most of the time, apparently looking forward only to meal times.

Hall gained two stone during the deathwatch, while Bonnie added nearly a stone to her already plump figure. Hall cared little about his appearance, often going days without shaving. Bonnie, however, fretted because she was not allowed a nail file. Guards obligingly set up a mirror, beyond her reach and outside the bars of her cell, so that she could adjust her hair and apply make-up.

Thousands of people wrote letters to the condemned couple, but Hall and Heady showed little interest in this avalanche of mail. After glancing at a few letters, they told the warden they didn't want to see any more. Bonnie filled in the time by doing crossword puzzles, and Hall read cowboy stories in magazines and books as fast as the guards could supply them.

A couple of weeks before their execution both kidnappers – without any communication between them – wrote almost simultaneously to Mr. Greenlease asking his forgiveness for the anguish they had caused him and Bobby's mother.

Carl Hall and Bonnie Heady showed remarkable resignation, fortitude and courage on Death Row. They seemed detached from the events going on around them, not caring what happened to them or what was going to happen. On the afternoon of December 17th, 1953, guards asked them what they would like for their last meal. By coincidence, each ordered exactly the same dinner: fried chicken, mashed potatoes and gravy, salad, rolls, Roquefort cheese and pineapple ice cream.

As a final concession they were allowed to eat this last meal together. A table was pushed into the corridor against the bars of Hall's cell, where Bonnie joined him. They spent about 30 minutes over the meal, chatting and smiling. At 7.30 p.m. Bonnie was returned to her cell.

At 11.32 they were driven in separate cars to the death house, although it was only a couple of hundred yards away. They met again in a detention cell and sat side by side on a narrow bed for their last brief conversation.

"I wish they had let us be married," Bonnie said.

"Yeah," replied Hall as he took a deep drag on his cigarette.

She was wearing a black cape she had borrowed from a prison matron. Underneath this was an apple-green cotton dress. She wore a pair of low-heeled sandals, but no stockings. Hall wore the regulation olive-green prison uniform, with black vertical stripes on the trousers. His wrists were manacled. Bonnie's were left free.

At last the warden came in and said, "It's time." They stood up and Bonnie threw her arms around her lover, pulling his head down to her so she could kiss him. When he straightened up, the red smear of he lipstick made him look like a clown, but he was unaware of this. Then the couple were blindfolded and led into the death chamber, sealed off by windowed walls from the observation room where 17 witnesses had gathered to see them die.

Attendants guided them into the twin steel chairs and made last-minute adjustments, tightening straps round wrists, chest and waist.

"It's too tight," Bonnie complained about a wrist strap. She joked: "Still, I'm not going anywhere." An attendant loosened the strap, and then buckled it again.

"Thank you," Bonnie said. She twisted her head this way and that. "I can't see a thing," she said, trying to peer out from beneath her blindfold. Turning towards Hall in the other chair, just two feet away, she asked, "Are you doing all right, honey?"

"Yes, mama," he murmured.

The attendants left the chamber, and then a US marshal came in. He bent close to Hall and asked if he had any last message. Hall shook his head. The marshal asked Bonnie the same question.

"No," she said. Almost as an afterthought, she added, "Thank you." She seemed pitifully eager to please.

The marshal left them and the doors swung shut and were sealed, leaving the doomed lovers alone under the gaze of the witnesses. Now their lips moved with a seeming urgency. Both appeared to be talking at once, but whether they were praying or speaking to each other no one will ever know. No one outside the death chamber could hear what they were saying.

For a moment the witnesses stared in hypnotised fascination. Then the warden moved a lever that released pellets of potassium cyanide into the crocks of sulphuric acid under the death chairs.

Yellowish fumes swirled up into the nostrils of the condemned couple and their heads fell forward, as if they had dropped off to sleep. For a few more moments their bodies convulsed, fighting the straps that bound them. Bonnie seemed to fight harder than Hall. Their heads jerked upwards in violent motion – Hall's mouth opened like a narrow gash; Bonnie's gaped wide, gasping for air.

A moment later they both slumped forward again, and a 12.12 a.m. on December 18th, 1953, Carl Austin Hall was pronounced dead. Two minutes later Bonnie Brown Heady was pronounced dead too. Her lipstick could still be seen through the observation windows, grotesquely smeared where she had kissed her lover for the last time.

He was probably smeared the same way the first time she kissed him, and either kiss could be called the kiss of death.

Bonnie Heady became the first woman in American history to be executed for kidnapping. She is known to have been a drug abuser, an alcoholic and to have had an impressive number of sexual partners. Not much else is known about her, but her sanguine attitude to her victim's death and her own execution poses a number of questions. Why, for instance, did she agree to have young Bobby murdered? Was she really as cold-blooded a killer as her lover?

Why did she fall for the sleazy jailbird anyway? Did she love him so much that she feared to lose him and agreed to anything, even becoming a child killer?

She points up one lesson for those who feel that the gentle sex should not pay the ultimate price for murder. Not all women are softies. Indeed, some of them are downright dangerous.

Judy Buenoano became the first woman executed in Florida for 150 years

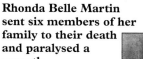

Rhonda Belle Martin sent six members of her family to their death and paralysed a seventh

Mary Frances Creighton was taken to the electric chair at Sing Sing by wheelchair

Women Executed In America 1900–2005

Eva Coo killed an alcoholic handyman so that she could collect his life insurance

Dovie Dean eats her last meal in her cell. She was only the second woman to be executed in Ohio's electric chair

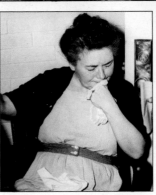

Louise Peete was overcome to hear that her husband had committed suicide after her arrest on murder charges

Women Executed In America 1900–2005

Annie Beatrice McQuiston aka "Toni Jo" smiled as she descended the stairway to the execution chamber at the parish jail. Below, Toni Jo awaits the verdict at one of her three trials

The Boxer's Mate

Barbara Graham thought she had bought herself a perfect alibi but he turned out to be an undercover police officer

San Quentin's gas chamber

A Murder For Nothing At All

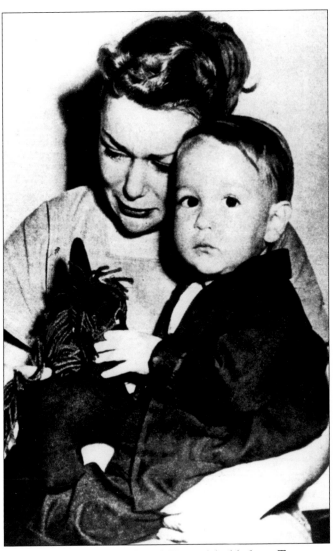

Barbara Graham on Death Row with third son Tommy

A Murder For Nothing At All

Ruth Snyder behind bars

On the last day of Anna Antonio's life, before she went to Sing Sing's electric chair, she said to her brother, "Let's pretend I'll still be here tomorrow"

"What Will Happen To My Children?"

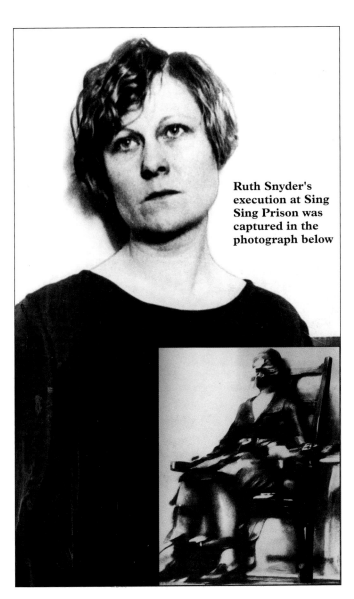

Ruth Snyder's execution at Sing Sing Prison was captured in the photograph below

Horror Of The Last Walk

Irene Schroeder and Glenn Dague were executed in the same electric chair in quick succession

The Trigger-Happy Waitress

PART THREE

1 – THE BOXER'S MATE
Annie Beatrice McQuiston

She was small and slim, with lustrous black hair worn in a shoulder-length bob. She was 24 but looked younger, despite the hardness in her seen-it-all eyes. Few people knew her real name. They just called her Toni Jo.

He was 27, tall, burly and dark. Known as "Cowboy" in the boxing ring, where he spent a lot of his time, he was a tough nut, always out of funds and always in bad trouble. The shuttered home from which they had just emerged had been Toni Jo's place of employment since she was a child. It was, in fact, the town's whorehouse.

"I'm going for a walk," Toni Jo told the henna-haired madam who stopped her as she approached the door.

The madam's lips tightened. Then, unexpectedly, she nodded her head. "OK, but only for an hour," she said. "Don't be late. There'll be plenty of customers coming in after the football game."

"I'll be back, don't worry," Toni Jo promised. She flung a light topcoat over her slim shoulders, making sure that it didn't quite conceal her alluring figure outlined by a clinging sweater and too-tight skirt. "Come on, Cowboy."

"What's your real name, honey?" Cowboy asked her a little later, as they talked over drinks in a bar on the San Antonio, Texas, main street.

"You first," she retorted pertly. "What's behind the name Cowboy?"

"Claude Henry," he told her. "Henry's the family name. Believe it or not, I once had a family and a home."

"Sure you did. So did I." Toni Jo sighed with sympathetic understanding. As they left the bar and strolled along the street in the gathering dusk, she told him that she had once been known as Annie Brown, but her real name was Annie Beatrice McQuiston. She was born in Shreveport, Louisiana, she went on, where the McQuistons were of some consequence. One of her relatives was a nurse; another was a high-ranking officer in the Louisiana state police.

"For crying out loud, honey!" Cowboy blurted out. "Don't you go messing me in with any cops!"

Toni Jo's eyes clouded. "Why, Cowboy? Are you in some kind of trouble?"

At that moment he saw the fear and appeal in her eyes and, although he had been on the point of confiding in her, he thought better of it and just shrugged. That could come later. Right now, there was another truth to be faced.

"It's getting late," he said. "I've got to be taking you back. You promised you'd only be out for an hour." He added bitterly: "If only I had the right kind of dough..."

Toni Jo snorted. "Never mind that," she said. "I had this figured. We've got dough right here, in the first national bank." She patted the top of her stocking and winked meaningfully. "I didn't leave that place tonight with a handbag because the old hag would have squawked – they guard the takings like it's Fort Knox. But I knew you weren't exactly in the chips right now, so..."

She lifted her skirt, peeled back the top of her stocking and pulled out a considerable wad of folding money.

She smiled as Cowboy's face flushed. For a moment she thought he was going to walk out. "Don't be like that!" she pleaded. "We're friends, aren't we? Anyone can help a friend. You can pay me back, Cowboy – every darned nickel if you want."

Cowboy's eyes bulged as she began to count off the greenbacks. When she had finished she said: "I've no intention of going back tonight, Cowboy. I brought this cash with me because we're going out on the town to have a darned good time."

For the next 72 hours they did just that, spending the dollars freely on anything that took their fancy, thoughtlessly, recklessly, lavishly. Toni Jo remembered long afterwards that she had never been so happy. She was in love with her Cowboy, and that for her was all that mattered in the world.

When their spree was over they rented a furnished room that would be their first home together. Several days later she went back at the shuttered house to collect some of her things and some money due to her – and to quit her job as the most popular inmate of the establishment. The hard-eyed madam at first exploded with rage, then pleaded with her. But Toni Jo shook her head. Her mind was made up. "He wants me," she explained. "And I want him. This is for keeps. And do you know what? He's promised to get me off drugs."

"He has, has he?" the madam sneered. "Well, while you've been enjoying yourself, I've been checking up on your Cowboy Henry. Did he tell you how many fights he ever won? He can count them on one hand. And did he tell you he's lugging round a bail bond heavier on his back than that monkey you're carrying?"

Alarmed, Toni Jo recalled Cowboy's brief reference to "messing with cops," but she didn't blink an eyelid. "Sure he told me all about that," she lied.

"So you know you've picked yourself a cowboy the courts ride hard on!" the madam snorted. "Your cowboy's been tried for murder!"

Toni Jo flushed. "As if I didn't know that!" she retorted. As she turned to stalk out of the shuttered house it seemed to her that the world was in free-fall around her. She hurried back to the furnished room to confront Cowboy.

"It's true," he said, hanging his head. "I stood trial on a murder charge and the jury found me guilty. I'm only free at the moment because my attorney appealed the verdict. He got me out under heavy bail."

"What happened? Toni Jo asked tersely.

Slowly, he told her the story. It began on an autumn night, November 16th, 1939. That was almost two years ago. He and a casual friend of his, Arthur Sinclair, a special policeman, had escorted two girls to a tavern. Sinclair was 34, much older than Cowboy Henry, and had become surly with drink. He said something about the girl who was with Cowboy that provoked a vicious argument. Sinclair stepped outside, and Cowboy followed him.

Right after that came the sound of a shot. A bullet whined past Cowboy's ear, fired from an ambush. He rushed at the lurking Sinclair, wrestling him to the ground and disarming him.

Then came a second shot. Arthur Sinclair died that night from a bullet fired from his own gun. And Cowboy Henry was accused of killing him.

The trial was held the following January, and the accused young boxer stuck to his story of the attempted ambush. He insisted that he had only taken the gun away from Sinclair and fired in self-defence, convinced that his assailant would get another weapon and try again to shoot him from behind.

This defence failed to impress the jury, which voted unanimously for conviction. But the appeal court granted Claude Henry's lawyers a new trial for their client, the judges ruling that the trial judge had inadequately instructed the jury. As a result, Cowboy was out on bail. The new trial was to come up next winter, and his attorneys had won their argument for a change of venue.

Toni Jo's brow puckered. "I don't like it," she said.

"But it's a cinch, honey. You tell them you feel you never can get a square shake in the court you've been in already, and you petition that they hold your next trial in another county, where no one knows you. They say it could be in Hondo, for me."

Toni Jo felt irritated by his optimism. "You should have told me all this before," she complained. "I suppose you took me for someone who'd quit you as soon as the going looked rough?"

"I was going to tell you and I put it off. Yeah, and the going is getting rough, as well as expensive."

There was a heightening tension between them, and they both knew why – she wanted a fix. "I told you, no more drugs," he said steadfastly. "We both agreed you've got to come off the junk."

She began to rage, and when she raged she was like

a tigress with unsheathed claws. He tried everything to dissuade her, but nothing worked. It was pure cold turkey – the worst kind. You just quit all of a sudden and sweat out the torment with no sort of tapering-off at all. It's a living nightmare.

Wearily, Cowboy took Toni Jo off to see a doctor. A knowing man, with half his practice on the fringes of the underworld, he gave her a sleeping draught and warned them of the dangers of cold turkey.

"It's not the best cure, and certainly not the safest," he said. "In your case I would definitely advise against it."

When she woke up Toni Jo was feeling better. Undeterred by the doctor's advice, she was determined now more than ever to give up narcotics. And amazingly she succeeded. Only a couple of months after decamping from the San Antonio whorehouse with her Cowboy she was free from all craving. It seemed to her that a whole new life lay ahead of her now.

They borrowed a car from one of his pugilistic pals and drove to Sulphur, Louisiana, a little town in her native state, where a justice of the peace married them – Claude Henry and his big bail bond taking for life Annie Beatrice McQuiston and her heavy past as Toni Jo, hooker. For the first time in five years she used her right name when signing the marriage register. As soon as Cowboy's second trial was over, they both agreed, they were going legitimate.

As a reward for shaking off the demon drug, Cowboy took his bride off to honeymoon in southern California. Throughout the holiday he had to keep in touch with his attorneys and his bail bondsmen. They were certain to get after him should he decide to switch from honeymooning tourist to fugitive and try to jump bail.

The crunch came after 10 days. Cowboy was handed a telegram summoning him to appear at Hondo, Texas, for his new trial – a trial for his life – in another 10 days' time.

"Don't go!" pleaded Toni Jo. "It was a frame-up – you killed him in self-defence. Now we're out here they can't extradite us anyway."

"They can, and they would," he replied. "They told me so before we left."

"Then we'll hide. We'll change our looks. Guys have often told me I'd look all right as a cute blonde."

"But I like you just the way you are." He shook his head emphatically. "It's not right, Toni Jo. I'm not leaving my bondsman holding the bag."

"We could pay your bondsman back. We can get the dough. Like, well, for instance, I can earn it." She assumed an inviting pose. "I've done it plenty of times before."

"Skip it! Those days are over. We got married, remember? I'm going back." He assumed a tone of unaccustomed gravity. "They say this change of venue is a lucky break. I'll tell my side of it and get acquitted – and the Henrys will live happily ever after."

And so they went back to Texas because, as Cowboy had said, not to do so would have been a terrible mistake. But after his arrival for the trial in Hondo things began to go pear-shaped.

On the witness-stand he was quiet and confident enough. But the evidence told against him. At the end of the hearing the jury foreman, a sandy-haired, weather-beaten man, stood up and replied to the judge's formal question: "Yes, your honour, we have reached a verdict. We find the defendant guilty of murder."

It was Saturday, January 27th, 1940, the darkest day of Toni Jo's scarcely roseate life. The judge, like the jury, had clearly been unimpressed by Cowboy's self-defence story, and he thought the boxer's punishment had been delayed quite long enough. He sentenced Claude "Cowboy" Henry to 50 years in the Texas State Penitentiary at Huntsville.

Toni Jo had listened to the verdict with some degree of composure, but the harshness of the sentence detonated something inside her. She leapt to her feet, swift and frantic, climbed over a low railing to evade a bailiff at the gate that separated the accused from the well of the court, swept aside the deputies surrounding the prisoner and on tiptoe clasped him against her pounding heart.

"You can't do this, ma'am!" a bailiff protested.

Toni Jo ignored him.

"Cowboy! Oh, Cowboy!" she cried. Her eyes shone with the fire of fierce resolve. "Don't you worry, Cowboy, I'll get you out! I swear it. I'll get you out!"

Sheriff's deputies pulled her away. "You can visit him, ma'am, just as soon as the law allows," she was told.

Before she went tearfully home that day, she conferred with her husband's attorneys. They had been supportive and persistent, but they now told her frankly that the appeal court, having once before set aside Cowboy's penalty, would be far less receptive to renewed petitions, particularly since the second trial had been conducted with impeccable fairness.

"Furthermore," one of the lawyers added, "the appeal procedure is expensive. Any further action initiated by you is going to cost a lot of money."

"Don't worry about the money," Toni Jo flashed back recklessly. "I can get the money."

Cowboy had already reached a decision at the start of his sentence. He was throwing in the towel. There would be no more appeals. As he was entrained to Huntsville he was resigned to his fate – the rest of his life in the penitentiary.

Toni Jo left Hondo that evening and went to Beaumont, a small town fairly convenient for the prison. She rented a room, from where she would be able to visit Cowboy regularly. This was a spur-of-the-moment plan, but she was already nurturing far more dangerous ideas.

For she knew Beaumont, and she had contacts there. She had begun to work the circuit in 1933, when she was 17, so she knew all the madams and girls who had been through every mill that warps and toughens humankind. In a frenzy of longing for her Cowboy, she turned to several of these seasoned campaigners to ask what she should do.

"Don't do nothing, kid. Not right away," one of them advised her. "You'll only hurt your guy's chances if you try to spring him too soon. Let the dust settle, for a year at least. Visit him regularly, always beg him to obey the rules, give no trouble and keep his nose clean. Then, for his good conduct, they'll move him to a prison farm. From there, you'll be better able to spring him.".

Toni-Jo promised to be cautious and wait. But she never meant to wait a whole year. And it was around that time that she met a young ex-convict of several aliases, who was introduced to her as "Arkansas," named after the state he hailed from.

Although he was only 23, Arkansas had already served a term for burglary in the Huntsville Penitentiary. When he was released, he joined the army. The day Toni Jo met him he was AWOL from Fort Sam Houston in San Antonio, and lying low to evade being recaptured.

Toni Jo decided that if anyone on the outside could tell her about the inside of Huntsville it was this young man. Quizzed about it, he said he knew the prison inside out. When she began to sell him on her hope for an early reunion with her husband the idea appealed to him because he was broke, on the run, in need of transport and looking for a profitable adventure.

"OK, I'd say we could spring your guy," he told her. "But you'll need a few things. You'll need dough – a big fat roll of it. And we've got to have a good fast car."

They began planning seriously. Arkansas soon told her about the nub of his proposal. Up in his native state he knew a little hick town near Camden, with a small but profitable bank, just begging to be robbed. The ex-burglar, ex-convict and ex-soldier had thoroughly cased the place on the one occasion he went home on leave.

"So there's our dough. And the fast car's easy to get hold of," Toni Jo said. "But, Arky, you can't afford to buzz around here in Beaumont, with the MPs looking out for you. But I'm in the clear, so I get us our guns."

She got the guns that same night – February 12th. Two agile teenagers, recommended to her by another underworld contact, listened to her problem, and then named their price of five dollars. For this, the teenagers broke into a hardware store and came out with an assortment of guns. There were .32 revolvers and .38 automatic pistols, together with a quantity of cartridges of both calibres.

Arkansas exulted over the guns when he called next day at the house where Toni Jo was staying. "All this for five bucks? For fifty, maybe, these kids would go and get your husband out."

He laughed. But Toni Jo didn't. Her eyes were glinting wickedly. Arkansas stopped laughing. He concluded that this confederate of his might turn out harder than any girl with her curves was entitled to be.

Two days after the weapons heist, on St. Valentine's Day, Toni Jo and Arkansas were set to pull out of Beaumont. When Arkansas called for her he grimaced at her bright red slacks and green jacket. "We'll be spotted for sure, with you in duds like that so easy to remember," he observed.

But her thinking was way ahead of him. She thrust a plastic bag under his nose. "See this bundle? I've got a plain little dress in it. After we hijack the car, I change into it. When the guy whose car we take tells the cops, he remembers this red and green outfit and they broadcast my description. But by then I'm dressed entirely differently. Get it?"

Arkansas agreed that she should be in charge of operations – at least until they reached the state of Arkansas and were ready to rob the bank. The fact was that in setting out to involve themselves in violent crime each felt lucky in teaming up with the other, though from different motives. Toni Jo was uncompromising and bossy, and few men would have willingly subordinated themselves to her. Arkansas, however, was easy-going. His main object was to get back into the state of Arkansas and hide there, out of the sight of the US Army.

The one motive they currently shared was getting as much as they could from the bank they were going to rob. To this end he took care of loading the guns – two of the .38 automatics for himself, and a nickel-plated .32 for her. Thus armed, they had various other guns and plenty of ammunition left over, a burden neither of them wished to carry. Toni Jo made the weapons up into a neat parcel, tiptoed up to the attic of the boarding-house where she was staying, and hid it where she might find it again in case the plan for springing her husband from jail went wrong.

The two desperados set off for the outskirts of Beaumont. They walked on to the New Orleans highway, Route 90, known locally as the Old Spanish Trail, and almost immediately a friendly motorist pulled up to offer the attractive girl and the inoffensive young man a lift.

Toni Jo murmured to her accomplice: "Not this car. It's too old. It isn't fast enough."

Arkansas nodded his assent, but they still smiled back at the driver and accepted his offer. They told him they were newlyweds, on their way to New Orleans. Rolling into Orange, a Texas town on the Sabine River across from Vinton, Louisiana, Toni Jo thanked their benefactor with a radiant smile. Would he kindly drop them off at the bus station? No problem, he said. He waved and tipped his hat. He was one of those typically good-natured Texans who wouldn't realise how lucky he had been until one day he read about it in the papers, and remembered the girl and the young man he gave a lift to.

Dusk had fallen and it was beginning to rain when Toni Jo and Arkansas stood at the edge of Route 90 again, signalling to eastbound motorists from the side of the highway.

"There – that's the one we need!' Toni Jo exclaimed suddenly.

A new green Ford coupé had slowed and stopped some 20 feet beyond where they were standing. The driver was well dressed, genial-looking, a big, rather thickset man of about 40. He swung the door open and, as they climbed in beside him, said something about the rain and it being a mean night to wait by the roadside.

"We're heading for New Orleans," Toni Jo told him.

"I'll take you as far as Jennings, in Louisiana," he replied. "I'm delivering this vehicle to a friend who lives in Jennings. He's a car dealer."

The Ford V-8 was brand new, he told them, and it had a great turn of speed. Since passing through Beaumont he'd pushed it up to 90 mph. The driver was decidedly pleased with himself and the Ford. Toni Jo gave her accomplice a light nudge in the ribs. She was sitting on the outside of the front seat with Arkansas between her and the unsuspecting motorist.

"Not many of the old bangers around these parts could pass a new Ford doing ninety," Arkansas said admiringly.

They drove through Vinton and then sped through several small Louisiana townships. Ironically, one of them was Sulphur where, only 11 weeks and four days before, Toni Jo and Cowboy were married. Making good time, despite the gloomy, overcast weather and the spots of rain, they reached Lake Charles, taking the winding highway route through the city. After that they broke out into open country again, leaving the towns and suburbs behind them.

Toni Jo gave Arkansas a hard nudge with her elbow. This was it...She drew her shiny .32 from where she was hiding it. Leaning forward, she pointed it so that the driver could see it clearly defined in the light from the dashboard instrument panel.

"What's the idea?" he began, instinctively putting his foot on the brake pedal.

Toni Jo rasped: "Just keep going, till I tell you where to stop." After a few minutes' silence they reached a crossroads and she ordered: "Turn left here."

Shocked and unnerved, the driver obeyed. They drove on in wary silence for another 10 minutes. "Stop!" Toni Jo commanded. The car came to a halt on the side of a lonely road. She scrambled out, while Arkansas, who had drawn one of his two pistols, kept the driver covered.

"Look, I've got fifteen bucks on me," the driver said. "Oh, yes – and this wristwatch. I don't want any trouble. You're welcome to them..."

"Thanks very much," Toni Jo said. "We'll take them. This is a stick-up, mister. We also want your car and your clothes."

"My clothes?" he quavered.

"You heard me! Get out of the car and get out of that

suit, or else I'll blow off the top of your head!"

The motorist didn't hang about after that. Shivering in the night air, he stood in front of the flint-eyed Toni Jo, hesitant to undress under her shameless gaze. "I can't see what you want my suit for," he whined. "It's much too big for your husband."

"Fat lot you know about my husband!" yelled Toni Jo. "He's as big as you and, right now, he's wearing a prison suit. I need your suit for him when we spring him."

It was an incredibly dangerous thing to say, because it committed the pair either to kidnap the innocent motorist or to silence him forever. But Arkansas didn't seem to think she had pushed herself too far. His concern was that they weren't in such an isolated place as they should have been. He nodded towards some nearby towering oil derricks, visible in the light of gas flares, and whispered: "Better get a move on."

Their victim had now undressed and stood shaking in his underwear. He handed his wallet and his watch, which he had unstrapped, to Toni Jo. She checked the wallet to ensure that there really were 15 dollars in it and handed the watch to Arkansas. Then she snatched up their victim's suit and tossed it into the car.

All this time she was pointing the .32 at him, intending to send him loping off into the night. But now she realised the error she had made by telling him that they were going to spring someone from prison. He could raise the alarm – if he found a cop he could even lead the police to the prison before they got there themselves. He didn't have far to go to get help – there must be oilmen working on those derricks not so far away.

She motioned him to get into the open boot of the car. When she slammed down the lid it caught his hand, crushing it agonisingly. He cried out in protest and pain, but Toni Jo didn't care. She just cursed him for being so awkward.

"What you gonna do with him?" Arkansas asked as he took the wheel.

Toni Jo slid in the seat beside him. "You drive. I'll think of something."

Soon they were crossing the federal highway again, heading south-east towards the Gulf of Mexico. After 40 minutes Arkansas braked and pulled in beside a line of haystacks. He asked her again: "What you gonna do with him? He's gonna be a big nuisance if we hang on to him."

"I'll march him to one of those haystacks," she said. "After I get him out of the boot you turn the car around for a fast take-off."

"What you gonna – "

"Just do as I say. I'm in charge. I'll attend to it!"

She got out of the car, opened the boot, and had to hold up her victim until he overcame the numbness of being confined in the tiny space.

"Get your underwear off, too," she said. "I might need it for my husband." She looked at his injured hand scornfully. "And don't get blood on it."

"I'll be naked," the shivering driver protested.

"You'll be walking in front of this gun, so you won't see me blush," she snapped back. "Anyway, in my profession I've seen more naked men than you've had hot dinners."

When he had stripped himself she marched him ahead of her across a field, well out of sight and earshot of any occasional passing car. When she told him to stop he gripped his throbbing hand and tried to make his voice sound steady. "I suppose you know you can get a long stretch in the penitentiary for this sort of thing?" he said

Toni Jo snorted. "Seeing where I'm sending you, mister, you'd better kneel down. You don't have a wish, but you can have a prayer."

The doomed motorist sank to his knees with a low moan. "I won't pray for myself," he said. "I'll pray for both for us."

She stood beside him, pointing the gun downwards at his head. The bullet tore into his skull, killing him instantly.

Behind her, several hundred yards way, Arkansas was turning the car round when he heard the shot in the distance. He shuddered involuntarily. All he wanted to do now was to get himself out of this mess. Never mind the girl. She was a trigger-happy killer. She'd have to find some other sucker to snatch her husband from the Huntsville pen.

He was just about to speed off when Toni Jo appeared at the car door, with the nickel-plated gun still in her hand. Arkansas knew that if he tried to make a getaway now, she'd put the other five .32 bullets into him.

He smiled as she got in. "So that's that," he said.

"Get going, Arky!"

He drove fast, taking a circuitous route towards the Arkansas state line. He drove though the night, stopping twice to buy petrol, paid for by Toni Jo with the murder loot of $15. It was almost dawn on February 15th when she told him he could stop and they could get something to eat.

Their immediate destination now was Camden and its bank. They would scout around the place first, sizing it up, before busting it. While they were breakfasting Arkansas asked, trying to sound indifferent: "Why did you want his suit and stuff? Was it really for your husband?"

"Yes," she said. "He can't very well go shopping for new clothes after we spring him. Besides, with that motorist lying there with nothing on, it makes it harder for the cops to identify him. It could be as much as a week before the alarm for this car is sounded. We'll be hundreds of miles away by then."

They arrived in Camden at 8 a.m., parked the car and went into a small hotel on the main street. They registered as Mr. and Mrs. Ray Johnson and, because they had no baggage, paid in advance. Overcome by fatigue from the night's exertions, they went straight to their second-floor room.

Toni Jo still carried her plastic bag of clothes. She hadn't changed from the vivid red and green outfit she was wearing, since the man whose car they had hijacked would now never be able to give a description of her.

Arkansas went to the window and looked down on the

main street, his mind buzzing with escape ideas. Toni Jo had slipped out of her clothes and was lying in one of the twin beds, covering her shoulders and dragging on a cigarette. He looked longingly at the other bed, desperate with fatigue, hardly able to keep his eyes open. But the urge to escape from all this was more overwhelming.

"You know, there might be an alarm out already for that car, since the guy didn't actually own it," he said slowly. "Perhaps it was a bum idea, parking it down there, so close to the hotel. It could bring trouble on us." He stretched and yawned. "I reckon I ought to go down and move it a block or two away."

"Sooner you than me, Arky," said the unsuspecting Toni Jo. "If I went down to move it undressed like I am, it could sure lead to big trouble."

Arkansas unlocked the door and disappeared down the hotel stairs. Toni Jo stretched, luxuriating in the warm bed. She crushed out her cigarette and fell back on the pillow. Within seconds she was asleep. When she woke she blinked around the room. She leaned out of the bed and turned the doorknob. Arkansas had left it unlocked, the key in the lock. She guessed instinctively what had happened, and cursed out loud.

She thought for a moment. How far would he run? Not to the cops, surely. She'd always suspected his loyalty to her. He was really just a sneaky rat.

What could she do now? Wide and viciously awake, she leapt out of bed and dressed, putting on the mousey-coloured outfit she had brought with her instead of the green and red one.

She walked down through the hotel lobby, and searched forlornly along the street for the green Ford, walking faster, growing angrier. You're wasting precious time, she said finally to herself; he's taken everything – the car, the clothes, the wristwatch and what was left out of 15 bucks.

A new plan, a fresh star, was needed urgently. The sight of a bus station across the street gave her a sudden idea. It was sheer impulse, and total deviation from her original plan to rob a bank for big money and spring

Cowboy. With most of the money she had left she bought a bus ticket from Camden to Shreveport, Louisiana. She had decided, in want and distress, to go home.

It was evening time when she got off the bus in Shreveport. Everything had a pleasant ring of familiarity about it, the shops, the side streets, the sleazy bars and dance places. She decided to walk to Hattie's place. Hattie had been her first madam. Hattie had taught her everything she knew about the game. Hattie was always shrewd, firm and kind. Hattie would tell her what to do.

She was convinced that Hattie would want her back. She had always been popular with the clients. Hattie would give her a room and an immediate income. After all, what were friends for?

Hattie received her with open arms and a warm welcome. "Good heavens, child, what have you been up to!" she cried. There were no sharper eyes in Shreveport than Hattie's. "I know all the gossip," she went on. "How you got married to a handsome young fighter, and how he took you off dope." She eyed Toni Jo up and down, then pointed to the bathroom. "You'd better get yourself cleaned up before you tell me all about it."

While Toni Jo took a shower and freshened herself up, Hattie glanced into her visitor's handbag. Almost no money, she noted, but a newish .32 revolver. She sniffed the muzzle, examined the cylinder. There were five live cartridges, one empty shell. The gun had been fired recently.

When Toni Jo was ready for warm food and steaming hot coffee, Hattie asked her: "Are you in some kind of trouble, honey?"

"I'm broke," Toni Jo confessed. "I need to start work here Hattie, right away. Tonight. I need some dough fast."

"You'll have to see the doctor first, honey. You know my rule. It's the same for any girl."

"But I'm married. I know Cowboy's in the pen, but —"

"Tell me all about it."

Hattie asked the questions and Toni Jo answered them dead straight. It was an even worse story than the exploded cartridge in the nickel-plated .32 had led the madam to expect.

"My girls live here, they don't hide," Hattie said at length. "I always liked your style, everyone thought you were hot stuff. But these days I barely pull enough custom to keep the house open. Times are hard, money's short." She looked defiantly at Toni Jo. She wasn't at all happy about that gun, and the trouble this girl might bring her. "Look, honey, you come from nice people in these parts. Ask them – they're bound to help you. There's your uncle, and your aunt. She's a fine, respectable woman. You must go and see her."

Toni Jo wouldn't hear of it. Her objections to throwing herself on the mercy of her family were loud and defiant. But Hattie had a way with her. She made it clear that this was the only direction to which she could turn for help. Hattie had been in business for years and she knew how to win arguments with obdurate women.

So, at length, late one evening Toni Jo went knocking on the door of her respectable aunt. She was received with all the generous show of affection that Hattie had predicted.

At the end of the day the aunt had only a vague and garbled account of her niece's St. Valentine's Day adventure, because she wasn't told about most of it. But next day she became increasingly disturbed by the hints and intimations in Toni Jo's story. Thinking it over, she decided to have a word with her brother, an officer with the Louisiana state police. That afternoon she went to police headquarters.

As it happened, her brother was out of town. She was about to return home when she was confronted by Sergeant Dave Walker, an old friend of her brother's. She decided that he must be the recipient of her misgivings.

Sergeant Walker listened to her story, and then thumbed through the inquiries and alarms that had come over the teletype recently. There was one in particular which he decided might be pertinent.

The previous day, February 15th, a woman named Eileen Calloway had appealed to police in Houston, Texas, on account of her missing husband, Joseph Calloway. It seemed that he had set out to do a good turn for a friend by delivering a new Ford car to a firm in Jennings, Louisiana. He had told his wife he would phone her from Jennings as soon as he arrived there. The phone call was important because he had promised to be back in Houston on Saturday, February 17th. That was his 42nd birthday, and his wife and their daughter were preparing birthday festivities for him. But Joseph Calloway, who worked at a department store in Houston, had neither phoned nor returned home.

Another call to headquarters was from the car dealership in Jennings, stating that they had not received their new car, being driven from Houston. Police reasoned that Calloway would have travelled over the much-used Route 90, and they checked with communities along that highway between his home and Jennings.

He had apparently stopped in Beaumont long enough to call on a friend – a service station attendant who he knew in Orange, Texas, remembered having served and spoken to the motorist before he drove on into Louisiana. They had discussed the new Ford and Calloway had remarked that despite the threatening bad weather that evening he expected to reach his destination within two hours.

He had driven on, presumably crossing the Sabine River, into Louisiana, and had vanished. An interstate alarm was out for him and now the authorities in Shreveport had received it, as had every other police post and sheriff's office in the state.

"I figure I'd better come with you, ma'am and talk to this young woman, " Sergeant Walker said gravely.

When her aunt arrived back with the police officer Toni Jo had composed her mind. She had decided to be truthful and candid, and tell her story to the police with no holds barred. She launched into the full panoply – her drug addiction, her cure and her marriage, her husband's "unjust" conviction and imprisonment and her determination to set him free.

When she came to the hitchhiking episode with her confederate and the shooting of the kneeling, naked motorist, a man who befriended them on a rainy night, her manner was so composed and casual that Sergeant Walker wondered if what she was saying could possibly be true.

"Where did you get rid of the gun?" he asked.

"I didn't. I've got it here," Toni Jo replied. She reached into her handbag and brought out the snub-nosed revolver.

Walker took the gun from her and spun the cylinder. Sure enough, one .32 cartridge had been fired. "Tell me about this fellow you call Arkansas. What is his real name?" he asked

"I don't know! And I don't want to know!" Toni Jo rasped, displaying more emotion that she had when she described the murder she had committed. "He was yellow right through, sergeant." Now, she thought, it was time for a bit of embellishment. "When he showed me what a punk he was, I slugged him with that gun. Knocked him cold and left him." It was a lie that wasn't likely to do her any good at all, but it probably made her feel better. She insisted that she had abandoned her unconscious accomplice in the car, on the road between Camden and El Dorado, Arkansas.

When Toni Jo's state policeman uncle reported back to Shreveport he found his niece in custody in a police cell. She recounted her incredible story to him with the same eerie composure. But at least as far as the police were concerned there was a yawning gap in her tale. When he phoned the police in Lake Charles he was told that no murder victim had been found in that area. And when he contacted Arkansas Police, they replied that the Camden to El Dorado highway was regularly patrolled and that no unconscious or injured man in a green Ford coupé had been found anywhere in the vicinity.

It was her uncle's harsh duty nevertheless to hand her over to his colleagues in the state police at Lake Charles. Captain John Jones, the commander there, asked her:

"Why did you do all this you claim to have done?"

"I did it for Cowboy. I'd do it again. I'd hang four times to get him out," she told him.

As she was being driven to Lake Charles she tried to direct her captors to the murder scene, but she wasn't able to pick it out. Next day, accompanied by Captain Jones and Trooper Fremont LeBleu, she retraced her journey along miles of country roads. She assured them that in daylight she would soon identify the haystack towards which she had prodded her shivering, defenceless victim.

It began to rain hard. When they were wet, these narrow back roads were treacherous. Visibility was reduced to a few yards, and Jones and LeBleu began to suspect that they were victims of a crazy hoax. Guided by Toni Jo's unsure sense of direction, they had frequently to leave the car and explore boggy fields of wet grass. They drew little comfort from the fact that she didn't seem to relish it much, either.

Once, returning to the car over sodden, squelching marshland, she snarled: "Damn that crummy fool. I would have put a couple more bullets in him if I'd known he was going to cause us all this trouble!"

LeBleu glanced over he top of her at his superior officer. Jones nodded. Anyone expressing thoughts as callous as that was probably not faking.

By early afternoon the little search party had explored everywhere, except for a region known as Plateau Petit Bois, around 12 miles south-east of Lake Charles. Here were plenty more dreary watery lanes. But Toni Jo seemed excited as she peered from the car window.

Suddenly she exclaimed: "There! That could be the place! Yeah, that's right where I told Arkansas to turn the car round." As the police car nosed slowly forward, she pointed to a haystack nearly 200 yards from the road. "That's the one!" she exulted.

The officers parked the car and hurried across the field with her. They saw the crumpled, decomposing body before they reached it.

Toni Jo still showed no remorse. She simply exclaimed:

"There, what did I tell you? And you thought I was just kidding you along."

The body of the naked man lay in front of the haystack, his knees still bent, just as Toni Jo had described the death scene. He had been shot once between the eyes, the bullet ranging downwards through his skull to the back of his neck. It was obvious that he had been shot while on his knees and that he had been kneeling below the gun muzzle. It was a classic execution murder. His left hand, crusted with blood, appeared to have been badly crushed.

Captain Jones summoned the owner of the field to stand guard over the dead body and they drove off back to Lake Charles. On the way, Toni Jo rummaged irritably in her handbag for a cigarette. "Gee, look!" she cried. "I forgot this." She held up a driving licence. "I got it from that guy's wallet when I nicked his measly fifteen bucks." She handed the licence to Captain Jones. It bore the name Joseph Calloway, of Houston, Texas – the man whose wife had reported him missing.

After the coroner had visited the site and looked at the body, it was removed to Lake Charles for a post-mortem. Close relatives of the victim came from Houston and made a conclusive identification. A ballistics expert established that the .32 revolver taken from Toni Jo had fired the bullet retrieved from the back of Calloway's neck.

A complete description of the hijacked Ford was teletyped to police all over the southern and southwestern states. The licence number on its Texas plates was N-10-754 and within a few hours a sheriff in Arkansas reported that the green car had been found abandoned at Arkadelphia. There were no fingerprints on the vehicle, but there were several cigarette butts stained with lipstick in the ashtray. There were bloodstains in the boot and a bundle of clothing, a suit and underwear to fit a fairly large man, was rolled up on the shelf behind the seat. Townspeople had noticed the car parked in the main street for some days, but no one remembered seeing the driver.

Toni Jo, locked up in a cell in Lake Charles since the discovery of Calloway's body, became uncommunicative and venomous. She refused to reveal the name of her accomplice, or to describe him, or to discuss the case any more. She lashed out at the cameras of newspaper photographers sent to take her picture until a deputy sheriff held her head, so that at least one glowering picture might be snapped. While she sulked in jail, insulting anyone who came to ask questions, flatly refusing to identify "Arkansas," police were putting together a picture of her life from information gleaned from files and friends.

Annie Beatrice McQuiston, as she truly was, was born on January 3rd, 1916, and when she was eight her mother, always ailing, finally succumbed to tuberculosis. Her father had been a railway employee, but left his job to become an oil company foreman, a position he soon lost because of his repeated drunkenness. He married again, and a new brood of children added to the poverty and discomfort felt by Annie's brothers and sisters.

Annie Beatrice ran away from home when she was 14 because she said she couldn't stand the poverty and the overcrowded living conditions. She didn't like school and when she went on to the labour market she didn't like working either. She became a prostitute in the town's brothel well before her 16th birthday.

Prostitution brought her into instant contact with drugs. For the next four years she lived with a succession of boxers, and got involved in a narcotics racket with one of them. Her police record in several states was significant – as Annie Brown, then as Toni Jo, she had been in trouble with the police eight times.

The first arrest was on August 6th, 1933, when she was 17. With two other prostitutes she was charged with "assault with a dangerous weapon" (this was a broken bottle) and with "wounding less than mayhem." But she was spared punishment because of her youth.

During the next four years she was arrested six times, on charges ranging from vagrancy, drunkenness and disorderly conduct to assault. Her drug addiction was now so serious that she was placed under a peace bond, at the request of another prostitute with whom she had been fighting. The complaining hooker testified that she was repeatedly threatened by Annie Brown and had good cause to fear for her life. Evidence given in court suggested that plenty of men also feared the girl they now called Toni Jo.

Her last serious brush with the law came in 1937, when she sold a quantity of mortgaged furniture, took the money and headed south-west with her then favourite boxer. She had only recently ventured back into her former haunts when she met Cowboy Claude Henry.

District Attorney Henry Pattison and Captain Jones studied her record and tried desperately to find something positive. "She looks bad through and through," Pattison said. "But this convicted murderer named Claude Henry seems to have been the one big thing in her life."

"If he was such an influence on her, one way we could get her talking again perhaps would be to bring them both together," Captain Jones mused. It seemed like a good idea, so, Cowboy Henry was approached. He agreed that if he were taken from Huntsville and allowed to see his wife alone, he would try to persuade her to do the right thing and tell the whole truth. So, after a complicated manoeuvre, Toni Jo was taken to Beaumont, Texas, to meet her husband.

The meeting took place in a private room in a city building so heavily guarded that there was no way either prisoner could make a break. After an agreed-upon interval, officers entered the room. They found Toni Jo sobbing in a corner.

"Cowboy says I got to tell you everything," she wept.

She proceeded to identify "Arkansas," her hitchhiker accomplice, as an army deserter and former convicted burglar who real name was Harold Finnon Burks. He told her that he had served a term in Huntsville in 1938.

Since the stolen Ford had been driven across state lines, the FBI now entered the case. They traced Burks to Warren, Arkansas, where he was living with his sister.

When police arrived at the house he was unarmed and offered no resistance. He told the FBI agents that he sold the two .38 automatics after fleeing from Camden and Toni Jo. He then drove to Arkadelphia, abandoned the Ford, and found a buyer for Calloway's wristwatch. Thus provided with funds, he took a bus to Warren, where he sought refuge in his sister's home.

"I was always afraid of Toni Jo," he admitted. "But she's lying when she says she hit me and left me unconscious in the car. She never hit me. She never knew, either, that I was fooling her all the time. I never had any intention of springing her husband from jail."

When they met for the first time in Beaumont, he went on, he was flat broke. He was an army deserter and he just wanted to get home. He figured he had a better chance of getting a lift if he went along with this flashy girl. So he deliberately encouraged her with his "inside" knowledge of the Huntsville penitentiary, brief though his stay there had been. He induced her to direct their course towards Arkansas with his sham story of the bank he claimed to have cased.

"If you really want to know something," he said, "that dame is a nut case. But she sure is one hell of a dangerous nut case."

Back in Lake Charles, Captain Jones quizzed Toni Jo on why she had claimed to have knocked Burks unconscious in the stolen car. She conceded that she hadn't done that. She agreed she had lied.

"And there's another thing I faked," she said. "I told you it was me who shot that guy Calloway. It wasn't me. It was Burks who took him to the haystack and plugged him. I couldn't help seeing it. But I never got out of the car."

Here was a new lie that seemed to have been suggested by her realisation that if she could shift the blame for the actual murder she might get away with a lighter sentence. It didn't make much difference for the moment, however, because Toni Jo and Harold Finnon Burks were both indicted for the first-degree murder of Joseph Calloway.

The court appointed two attorneys, Norman Anderson

and Clement Moss, to defend Toni Jo, and she wouldn't have been defended better if she had hired the best lawyers in the land. They were instrumental in obtaining a severance, which meant that she was tried before Burks, a position that was particular advantageous to her case.

Her trial began on March 27th, 1940. From the outset she was a pitiless perjurer, taking the witness-stand to shift all the blame and swear away Burks's life. He was the killer, she insisted. She had suggested stripping their victim naked, only in order to prevent pursuit.

She wanted to tell the court all about her deprived childhood, poverty that drove her into prostitution, but Judge John Hood declined to allow it. "All that has nothing to do with this murder," he said.

The jury talked it all over for seven hours, and it was clear that they didn't believe Toni Jo's story. They found her guilty and she was sentenced to death. Burks, in his subsequent trial, was convicted just as quickly, and he was also sentenced to be executed.

But on November 4th, 1940, the state supreme court granted Toni Jo a new trial, on the grounds that Judge Hood had permitted prejudicial conduct in the courtroom. At the same time Burks's execution was stayed, so that he could testify against Toni Jo.

The second trial began on February 3rd, 1941. Burks was the prosecution's star witness, and Toni Jo was again found guilty. But her two determined attorneys, fighting every inch of the way, appealed against the death sentence on 19 separate counts, and won.

Still another trial was granted to her, and for the third time she was found guilty and heard the death sentence pronounced. When the case was taken to the supreme court of Louisiana, that court upheld the conviction and sentence.

It must have seemed that attorneys Anderson and Moss had tried everything on behalf of their client, but they still weren't beaten. They found an obscure loophole in the wording of the 1940 state law, which decreed a change in Louisiana's execution method from hanging to death in the electric chair. It was just enough upon which to lodge another appeal, which they promptly did.

Meanwhile, Toni Jo, on Death Row in Lake Charles Jail, was allowed to keep a small black and white dog as a pet.

The high court finally ruled that the electric chair in Louisiana was constitutional. At that, Governor Sam Jones signalled that the case must come to its logical conclusion. He let it be known that he would refuse any clemency plea made to him on Toni Jo's behalf. She would have to die, and the date would be Saturday, November 28th, 1942.

She took her fate squarely on the chin and presided over a flamboyant press conference. Much of what she had to say was inevitably a rather amateurish eulogy of her relationship with Claude Henry. "That guy is king of my heart," she shrilled. "No one ever cared about me until he came along. Every man wants a passionate woman, but few are willing to risk marrying them, and Cowboy did just that. He took the monkey off my back, and I'll always be grateful to him for it."

The press conference also revealed a marked lack of remorse. "Most folks wonder what goes on in the mind of someone on Death Row. In the first place, the victim doesn't return to haunt me. I never think of him. I've known all along it would be my life for his. I believe mine is worth as much to me as his was to him. Sometimes I wonder why I didn't just knock him senseless. But it was like being drunk, real drunk. Ever pull something when you were drunk – and that something seemed the cutest, smartest thing in the world, and it was really the awfullest? Well, me, I was drunk with pressure."

The hacks duly scribbled down these bits of nonsense, but they had a better story when Toni Jo suddenly tried to offset two years of perjury by preventing the execution of Harold Burks. At each of her three trials she had declared under oath that he, and not she, was the real killer. Eight days before her scheduled date of execution she dictated and signed this retraction:

"I, Annie Beatrice Henry, fired the shot the killed J. P.

Calloway. It is my hope that Harold Finnon Burks will not have to suffer the death penalty."

Three days later, on November 3rd, there was a spectacular development. Cowboy Henry was transferred from Huntsville to the Central Prison Farm No. 2, near Sugar Land, Texas, when he was assigned to work in the laundry. This was like a British open prison, and allowed considerable freedom to the prisoners. When a small truck pulled up in front of the laundry building at around 11 a.m. that day, Henry and another prisoner named Clyde Byers clubbed the driver and made off in the vehicle, smashing through the prison farm gate and speeding off towards Houston, 25 miles away.

A general alarm was immediately sent out. Questioning other convicts, prison officers learned that Cowboy had become highly agitated after reading Toni Jo's farewell interview. He remarked to several of them that she was only in trouble on his account, and he intended to break out and somehow try to save her from execution.

Authorities at Lake Charles were told about the escape and a special guard was put on duty all around the prison where Toni Jo was on Death Row. That night, floodlights were set up to focus on the prison, and crack marksmen were placed in positions where they could survey every foot of the building.

When Toni Jo heard bout the escape, she exclaimed: "He's crazy if he thinks he can get me out of here." But all that night she kept vigil at the window of her cell, ready to yell a warning if he should rashly attempt a storming operation.

That afternoon Houston Police were given a tip-off from a prisoner at the prison farm. Cowboy Henry, it emerged, had said that if Toni Jo died he would kill the judge who sentenced her. It appeared that he could now be on his way to Lake Charles to kidnap Judge Hood, the first Toni Jo trial judge, or Judge Pickerel, who presided over her second and third trials. Guards were placed round the homes of both jurists, and members of their families were forbidden to go out without a police escort. That night Lakes Charles and the area all around it resembled an armed camp.

Next day, police in Beaumont heard that Cowboy Henry had been seen in the town. If this were true, it meant that he had closed the gap between himself and Toni Jo from over 200 miles to 66 miles. That was no mean feat, with a large segment of eastern Texas hunting him.

Detectives began covering every cheap hotel and boarding-house in the region. Eventually they arrived at a shabby hotel near Beaumont railway station. The sleepy-eyed manager snapped awake when they thrust a photograph of the fugitive in front of him.

"That sure looks like the guy who registered here tonight!" he exclaimed. "He came in after dark and…"

Radio calls were already summoning reinforcements. Men armed with submachine-guns suddenly appeared from nowhere. But when a detective rapped on the suspect's door, it opened, and he stepped out, both arms raised. It was Cowboy.

"Don't shoot," he pleaded. "I haven't got a gun."

As handcuffs were snapped on his wrist a police officer rapped: "Where's Byers?"

"I separated from him in Houston," he said. "I was aiming to get to Lake Charles to free my wife, and he didn't want any of that."

As they drove back to Huntsville, a maximum-security prison to which any prison farm escapee would automatically be re-committed, he pleaded for a chance just to say good-bye to Toni Jo. And back at Lake Charles, she was begging the authorities for a chance at least to speak to him on the phone. "This is like Romeo and Juliet," declared the Huntsville prison warden grimly. But the South is a sentimental place.

Two days after his re-capture, Cowboy Henry waited in the warden's office at Huntsville. The phone rang. Toni Jo was calling, from the chief jailer's office in Lake Charles Prison. This was her goodbye from Death Row.

Cowboy wept throughout the brief conversation. But Toni Jo, bright and encouraging, chided him for his foolish escape and begged him: "Get rid of that prison suit and go out the front door. Go straight and try to make something of your life. " She ended: "So long, honey."

She was still trying to help Harold Burks, again protesting his innocence. But this was to no avail. Four months later, on March 23rd, 1943, Burks was executed for the murder he had sat by and seen committed, but probably didn't think would happen.

Toni Jo astonished her guards by her cheerfulness after that last phone call to Cowboy. Her only complaint came on execution day, when her head had to be shaved. "Couldn't I wear a scarf for my execution?" she was asked. She was given permission to wear a gay bandana.

Her last request was to hear the latest episode of the radio serial Abie's Irish Rose, of which she was an avid fan. She wanted to know what happened next because, she said: "I'm scared. I don't know where I'm going, but it'll be good to know what Rose and the rest of them will be doing after this is over." Permission was duly granted.

At the end, she fell on her knees and prayed, just as the unfortunate motorist she murdered had done. At 12.12 p.m. the big lightning bolt of the law in Louisiana struck and ended her life, wasted for the sake of a senseless and callous crime.

2 – A MURDER FOR NOTHING AT ALL
Barbara Graham

The killers, hoods, and thieves involved in the murder
of 62-year-old crippled widowed Mabel Monahan were
a barbaric crew by any accounts. And they take a bit of
sorting out.

The facts are superficially clear. Mabel had a horror of
burglars. Perhaps that was because she had formerly been
the mother-in-law of Luther Scherer, a multi-millionaire
Las Vegas gambling boss. One of the stories prevalent
in Burbank, Los Angeles, where old Mabel lived in the
early 1950s, was that Scherer had stashed $100,000 or
more gambling profits in a secret safe at her home.

That's the sort of story that eventually finds its way
into the underworld and sets foul deeds in motion.

Which is undoubtedly why, on March 11th, 1953, a
gardener found the body of Mabel Monahan, who was a
former vaudeville star, crumpled in a hall cupboard in her
big white home on West Parkside Avenue in Burbank's
elite Mountain View district. The fragile, grey-haired old
lady had been savagely tortured, beaten and choked to
death while her hands were trussed behind her. She had
been dead for two days when her body was found.

The interior of her house was literally torn apart as
though the killer, or killers, had been frantically searching
for something. Yet valuable jewellery in her handbag was
untouched.

Who could have done this? Police sensed a connection
between the murder and the gambling rackets. Then
an informer told them that two former aides of Luther
Scherer's principal rival had had their eyes on the
rumoured hoard kept in Mabel Monahan's house. They
were Baxter Shorter, a 43-year-old ex-convict, and Bill
Upshaw, a 34-year-old gambler.

"They actually tried to get me involved," the informer
said. "But Upshaw got scared and kept putting off the
job. I had a row with Baxter and I pulled out. When
I read that Mrs. Monahan had been bumped off, I

thought I'd better come clean."

Baxter and Upshaw were brought in for questioning. Upshaw cracked first. Nervously assuring the officers that he hadn't been in on the actual murder, and given a promise of immunity and secrecy, he told what he knew.

"The leader of the murder mob was Jack Santo," he said.

Californian police knew all about Santo. He was a killer whose police record dated back to 1924. He had been arrested for kidnapping, suspicion of robbery, burglary and other offences.

John Albert Santo, to give him his full name, was a powerful, hard-faced man of 48 who stood 6ft 1in and weighed 14 stone. Of Spanish ancestry, he was ruggedly good-looking. He had arrogant ice-blue eyes behind shell-rimmed glasses, a pencil-line moustache and a debonair, masterful manner.

Estranged from his latest wife, he had been living for the past four years with Harriet Henson, a rough, lynx-eyed woman of 30. Big Jack often strayed, but he always came back to Harriet. He was currently facing a $100,000 lawsuit for savagely beating a man who made an offensive remark about the brunette.

According to Upshaw, Santo picked up on the story of the hidden cache at Mabel Monahan's home. Santo also quickly learned that he, Upshaw, together with Baxter Shorter, were both interested in it. Again, according to Upshaw, Santo then moved in to take charge of the operation.

Santo, it seems, had a chief lieutenant known only as "Perk," and another accomplice known only as John. He also brought into his mob a shapely young, reddish-golden blonde named Barbara. Her part in the raid was to induce the timid widow to open her door,

The job was set for the night of March 9th. Upshaw was originally scheduled to go along, but he was allergic to violence, he claimed, and not liking the look in Big Jack's eyes, he backed down at the last moment. Next day Baxter Shorter, who had been posted outside the house as lookout, told him what had happened.

Shorter said that when he went into the house he found Jack Santo, Perk and Barbara beating and torturing Mabel Monahan to make her reveal the hidden safe. They failed to find it and fled, leaving the trussed-up widow at the point of death.

With Upshaw's information in hand, detectives soon persuaded the jittery Baxter Shorter to talk, on a similar promise of immunity.

"I was there all right," he acknowledged. "But I don't go for murder. I'll tell you what happened."

Like Upshaw, he knew Jack Santo's mobsters only as Perk, John and Barbara. Shorter said he had worried about having a woman on the job, but Big Jack assured him that Babs, as they called her, was OK – that "she knows what happens to squealers."

As Shorter told it, Barbara went to the door and got the apprehensive Mrs. Monahan to open it by asking if she could use her phone. The others piled in while Shorter kept watch outside.

When they called him inside to help look for the safe, Shorter said, he was horrified to see Barbara beating the moaning widow over the head with her gun. Perk was also hitting her. Shorter, who hadn't bargained for violence, got out fast. On his way home, he put in a call for an ambulance, but in his anxiety he gave the wrong address.

Detectives soon identified Big Jack's accomplices. Perk was Emmett "The Weasel" Perkins, who had spent more than half his 44 years in prison for bank robbery, burglary and car theft. The blonde was Perkins's girl friend, Barbara Elaine Graham, a 29-year-old sometime prostitute and junkie with a police record up and down the West Coast dating back to 1937. John was John True, 38, a deep-sea diver.

All three had dropped out of sight, however, which led detectives to suggest to Baxter Shorter that he ought to have police protection. Shorter was disdainful. "I'm not afraid of a few punks who beat up and killed an old woman," he said. It was a sadly misplaced piece of bravado. A few nights later Baxter Shorter was kidnapped from his apartment at gunpoint by a snarling little man whom Shorter's wife identified positively as Emmett Perkins. Shorter was whisked away in a car with another man at the wheel.

His buddy Bill Upshaw hastily decamped just in time to Mexico. The only man the police laid hands on was John True, who denied any part in the murder. With no one to testify against him, he was released.

The fugitives were finally traced through some dud cheques issued by Barbara Graham. On May 4th a small army of Los Angeles police closed in on their hideout in a boarded-up building in the suburbs. They found Big Jack Santo almost naked, half asleep, lying on a bed. Perkins was in another room and blonde Babs was wandering around in a state of semi-undress. All three surrendered without resistance.

Booked on suspicion of murder, the hardened, con-wise trio wouldn't give the police the time of day. They denied ever knowing Baxter Shorter or Bill Upshaw, much less Mabel Monahan. Barbara Graham scornfully rejected offers of leniency if she would confess and implicate her companions. This was another sadly misplaced piece of bravado. She may not then have imagined that this was the last chance to save her life, but if she had known what she would later have to face, she surely would have squealed.

Santo, Perkins and Barbara Graham were brought to court in Los Angeles. Barbara's red-gold hair was braided in a double halo at the back of her head. She wore no make-up, other than a little powder and carmine lipstick. Her look was both defiant and demure. She wore a flowered print dress that hugged the smoothness of her hips and accentuated the fullness of her breasts. She sat next to her lawyer and clasped her hands in front of her.

Prosecutor Adolph Alexander outlined the gruesome story to the jury. "A blood-soaked pillowcase was pulled over Mrs. Monahan's head and face. Her wrists were bound with a strip of torn bed sheet – and another strip was knotted around her throat.

"Murderers of this type are not hatched in the churches, or in the homes of our community. They are spawned in the foul caves they infest. By night, they crawl out to perform their evil deeds. There are many Mrs. Monahans in this world, in the sunset and twilight of their lives. They are entitled to live in peace and sanctity of their homes. But there are a lot of Perkins and Santos and Mrs. Grahams who persist in crawling out from under slimy rocks.

"The dead voice of Mrs. Monahan cries out for justice from her grave. The entire state cries for justice.

"We will show that failing to locate this hidden hoard of money, these three people killed the old widow in cold blood, rather than leave behind a witness who could point an accusing finger at them."

Jack Santo smiled complacently as he listened to all this. He certainly wasn't worried. No once could deny that old Mrs. Monahan was dead. The fireworks would come later, when the DA would try to pin the blame on the three defendants. They would certainly need Baxter Shorter for that. And Santo knew that Shorter was well and truly dead. He had seen to it himself.

What Santo didn't know however was just how much Bill Upshaw had revealed to the cops. Upshaw knew the members of the gang. And because he wasn't on the job, his evidence might well provide the independent corroboration demanded by Californian courts, which would pave Santo's last mile to the gas chamber.

When he heard Upshaw's name mentioned by the prosecutor he began to sweat. Then, on an inspiration, he framed an alibi to save his own skin. His common-law wife, Harriet Henson, could fix him up with a woman who would swear that on the night of the murder he was shacked up with her in a hotel somewhere in Fresno.

But the prosecutor had an ace up his sleeve – John True was now willing to testify and his evidence would demolish any faked alibi. He was brought to the witness-stand on August 25th, and readily admitted that he knew Santo. He recalled a meeting in a motel where Santo introduced him to Emmett Perkins, Barbara Graham, Baxter Shorter and Bill Upshaw.

During the meeting Santo remarked that he must use dynamite in his work as a deep-sea diver, and could he use it to crack a safe? "I told him that was something I never did."

Later they went for a drive in Burbank and passed a house in Parkside Avenue. Perkins said: "That must be the place." True told the court: "I asked Santo what he was up to, what it was all about. He said people were hiding black-market money in a safe in that house and that all of us were going to get it. I agreed to go along with it only after he swore to me that no one would get hurt."

On the raid he followed the others into the house and immediately saw Barbara struggling with the widow in the doorway. "Mrs. Graham was lambasting the old lady in the face with her gun. She had her by the hair with her left hand and was striking her with the right. I told Barbara to cut it out, and put up my hand to stop her. The old lady collapsed.

"Pretty soon Barbara put a pillowcase over the old lady's head. Then Perkins came in and said, 'Let's get her away from the door.' He tied her hands behind her and dragged her by the feet up the hall till he got in front of a closet. Santo took a strip of cloth and tied it around Mrs. Monahan's face over the pillowcase. She was moaning, like she was hurt bad."

They all searched the house but found nothing. He went back to Mrs. Monahan, who was moaning.

"I'm a deep-sea diver, so I know how it's like to be down there with too little air," True explained. "I cut a piece out of the pillowcase, so she could breathe just a little more easily."

On the quiet, he said, he had told Baxter Shorter to call for an ambulance. It subsequently transpired that when Shorter fled the scene, he gave the emergency desk the address, but forgot to say it was in Burbank. That night the ambulance crew searched for the address in Los Angeles.

That night, True said, Santo drove him home. The two men talked about the possibility of the crime being laid at their door. "Sniffing gas in that chamber is an awful way to go," True said. Santo nodded. He said: "Don't forget there's two ways to go. If they catch you, you die. If you squeal, you die, too."

After Bill Upshaw took the stand and added his testimony, Santo and Perkins wee looking distinctly uneasy. Only Barbara Graham seemed serene, listening more as an interested spectator than as a defendant.

Her ace was that she had an alibi. She had met a woman friend in prison named Elsa who had agreed to help her by asking a friend on the outside, Sam Sirianni, to come to court and state that on the night of March 9th he and Babs were engaged in a cosy session in a motel room. Sirianni would produce a receipt for that night provided by an obliging receptionist. The whole deal would cost Barbara $25,000.

Barbara's first big shock, the first realisation that the alibi was about to be destroyed, was when Sam Sirianni was brought to the stand not for the defence but as a prosecution witness. The reason was soon clear – he was an undercover police officer who had posed as an underworld fixer. He knew Barbara's friend Elsa rather more than Barbara did, and Elsa had agreed to set up Barbara when the alibi proposition was put to her.

Barbara positively reeled as she listened to Sirianni's testimony, detailing their conversations, all captured on the police officer's hidden recording device. Barbara had talked freely to Sirianni about her involvement in the murder, and about Santo, Shorter and True too. After that, there was no hope for the trio. All were found guilty of first-degree murder, and on September 25th, 1953, all three were sentenced to death.

Eight months later Santo, Perkins and Harriet Henson wee brought back to another court to be tried for the murder of supermarket proprietor Guard Young, killed after he had collected the Friday staff payroll from his bank. Young had given a lift to four children on that day, and the trio had butchered all five of them. Santo and Perkins were again sentenced to death, and Harriet Henson was given life imprisonment.

Barbara, meanwhile, was locked up in Corona Prison before being transferred to San Quentin's Death Row. She was allowed to correspond with Stuart Palmer, a freelance writer who was present at her trial and had written a great deal about her case, and her letters to him reveal a calm and collected prisoner.

On February 25th, 1954, she wrote:

"Dearest Stu. Your letter arrived today. As usual, I'm so glad to hear from you.

So you went up to the Ventura School for Girls and checked up on me and my mother's record there! So Helen Coad is assistant matron now – isn't she a large, pleasingly-plump woman with a sweet-tooth? Send her some candy for me, and tell her hello for me. I'm sorry that I'm not one of her graduates to be proud of.

When I came here to Quentin, there were four of us condemned people here in this wing of the old hospital. By the time you receive this there will be one, me. Another execution tomorrow. It's not publicly announced, of course, but everybody knows.

That's all for this time, Stu. Thanks for everything. Will write you more later, because a girl in this fix just has to have somebody to talk to now and then. Best to your family, and hold them close.

Always the same, Barbara."

In her last letter to Palmer, dated March 1st, 1955, she continues to deny all involvement in the murder, which is curiously at odds with what she has apparently already told, or is about to tell, the San Quentin warden, as we shall see. She also expresses her weariness with the US appeal system for Death Row inmates – she has now been in prison for 18 months awaiting death. This is the letter:

"Dear Stu, I guess this is maybe the last letter I will ever be able to write to you, but I wan to say how much I appreciate

all your efforts on my behalf, and how much I wish that you really would say once out loud that you believe in my innocence.

I wasn't there! I didn't kill poor old Mrs. Monahan and I don't even know who did.

But the prospects are not good, and getting worse by the minute. I don't know how much longer Al Matthews can put up the dough for the cost of appeals and things – and they can only appeal on minor technicalities, anyway. Legal twists, that's all.

Meanwhile, life goes on, but sluggish. I play my records over and over. I eat sometimes, without tasting anything, and I sleep and doze and sleep again, but at night I mostly don't sleep. This is a period in which I guess I'm supposed to review my whole life, like a drowning man is supposed to do. But I'm just too tired and too bored.

I don't eat enough and I don't exercise. I am just a clam that crawls back to its shell and stagnates. Just waiting. But I still want to go free, or get the business. I cannot look forward to most of my lifetime behind bars. You yourself say you can get itchy and nervous when you are in prison for a few hours, even though you know you can get out any minute. How do you think I feel? As if you didn't know!

I'm beat, kid. I don't care what they do, only I want it over with. You asked me once if I could remember anybody, I mean any law officer, or matron, or stuff like that, who had ever in my long career taken time out to try to make friends with me and help me change directions. Not once. Really not one time. Nobody ever gave a damn, except the Good Sisters, years ago, and I should have stayed with them – and of course Hank, and some of the boys on the other side of the fence, who were always quick with a $20 when a girl needed it.

But I'm so alone. Nobody is so alone as I am. This goes on and on and never stops. Jack Hardy and Al Matthews and Bill Strong [her lawyers] have done their best and I guess they are still doing it, without a thin dime of pay. But in the appeal to the Supreme Court, what have they got to say except the minor stuff about the prejudice of the press and all that? I'm not kidding myself – I'm not going to get a new trial.

And I don't think I could live through it, even if I got one.

Sharon and some others of my family come to see me quite regularly. Hank comes sometimes. They will tell you hello from me. I wish I could see you, and keep on getting your letters, even if you kid me sometimes.

I'm sorry to hear that your cocker got run over, but you still have your cats and your children and your home. Go and see Mam and Tommy [her son] sometimes, and give him a big hug from me. I wish I could see him grow up. But I won't, so what's the use of wishing – of thinking? The best to you, always.

Love, Barbara.

On June 2nd, 1955, the day before she was due to die, Barbara was suffering from severe toothache. She didn't take any solid food all day. For her last meal she asked for a dish of ice cream. When she was taken to the special cell she had to walk past the death chamber where she was due to be gassed 19 hours later.

Given a sedative for her throbbing jaw, she changed into a pair of scarlet lounging pyjamas, and then began preparing herself for her fast-approaching end.

She was about to become the third woman to be executed in the history of California. Since there was no accommodation for women prisoners at San Quentin, the sprawling prison on San Francisco Bay, she was put in a special apartment just a few feet away from the death chamber. There she told Warden Harley Teets that she would talk to no one but her attorney and Father Dan McAlister, the prison chaplain.

She refused a chicken dinner brought to her cell and commented wryly to Warden Teets: "Why waste good food on me? Give it to someone who can enjoy it."

Through the long night the light burned in her cell as she prayed with Father McAlister. Phone lines were kept open to state governor Goodwin Knight's home in Sacramento. At 2 a.m. the governor's phone rang. The call wasn't from the prison – it was from William Strong, one of Barbara's lawyers. He was raising a legal point that Governor Knight thought worthy of consideration.

The governor promised him an opportunity to present the point to the state supreme court in Los Angeles later that morning. He also told the lawyer that he would alert Warden Teets of an impending stay of execution.

By five past nine that morning Barbara was making her final preparations in her cell for her 10 o'clock appointment with death, unaware of the legal arguments going on 500 miles way in Los Angeles. She laid out the stylish beige suit she had worn at her trial, showered, dressed, applied her make-up and meticulously groomed her hair. The only jewellery she wore was a gold wedding ring and a pair of shimmering rhinestone earrings.

Fifteen minutes later she was told that there would be a delay in order to give the supreme court time to consider the petition now before it. For the next hour she wavered between hope and despair.

At 10.27 the governor phoned the prison warden to tell him that the petition had been rejected. He added: "There is nothing further in my office, or before me, to prevent the carrying out of the sentence."

Barbara was now told that she would enter the gas chamber at 10.45. But with just five minutes to go a new writ was filed in the state supreme court. She was in fact on her way to the death chamber when she was told, at 10.44, that there would be another delay.

Her eyes brimmed with tears as she turned to Father McAlister and, clutching the sleeve of his black cassock, sobbed: "Maybe they've found out I'm innocent?"

She was led back to her cell, where she remained until 11.10. At that point the warden told her that the new petition had been rejected, and she would enter the gas chamber at 11.30.

Barbara broke down and wept disconsolately: "Why do they torture me like this? I was ready to die at 10 o'clock!"

By the time she again set out to walk past the newsmen in the waiting room, she had regained her composure. She stepped into the chamber and asked for a blindfold.

"I don't want to look into people's eyes," she told the guard, referring to the shocked faces of the newsmen, not five feet away from the gas chamber window.

A black stethoscope that was to be connected to the gas gauge outside the chamber was taped to her chest. Her lips moved in prayer as she was strapped to the chair and told to count to 10 before taking a deep breath. Finally, she was left alone in the locked death cell.

At 11.34 cyanide fumes began filling the chamber and her head dropped to her chest. Most of the witnesses were certain she was dead. One, journalist Seymour Ettman, remembered afterwards: "I was relieved she had died quickly and easily after a long, nerve-shattering delay. But I was wrong.

"For in a moment of horror that sent shivers down my spine. Barbara slowly lifted her head. From the strained, piteous look on her face, it was clear she was holding her breath in a frantic attempt to cling to life just as long as she could.

"I watched with growing terror, until she could hold her breath no longer. Then, with what seemed to be a sigh of despair, the breath burst from her lungs and, a second later, she gulped in the lethal fumes that snuffed out her life."

The prison doctor reported that she died "easily" at 11.42. By 2.30 p.m., when the lethal green chamber had been aired out, Jack Santo and Emmett Perkins were strapped side by side in the twin chairs. Sneering and defiant, they kept their grim secrets intact to the end.

"Don't do anything I wouldn't do," Santo joked to the warden. Perkins "the weasel" succumbed quickly. Big Jack died fighting for breath.

Barbara Graham's body, claimed by a woman friend, was interred at San Rafael. No one claimed the bodies of the two men, so they were sent to a state hospital for cremation.

The bloody curtain was thus run down on a catalogue of savage murders. But the aftermath of the Santo-Graham story continued for a long time.

Barbara had cursed and prophesied early death for those who wanted her death. She had threatened: "All the rats, all the liars, all the ones who want me dead will pay." And soon after her execution, a parade of deaths began.

No one gave it much thought when her original court-appointed defence counsel Jack Hardy, 51, who had left the case in disgust when her lying alibi attempt was exposed, died of a heart attack just one month after the execution. A year later, in October, 1956, her nemesis, District Attorney Roll, died of cancer at 52. In August, 1957, death by apoplexy stuck down Luther Scherer, the innocent bystander whose mythical $100,000 cache sparked the murder of Mabel Monahan.

Next to go was the man who, in a strictly literal sense, was directly responsible for Barbara's death, even though he had no relish for the task his duty imposed upon him. He was San Quentin's Warden Teets, who died suddenly of a heart attack on September 2nd, 1957, aged 50.

The deaths of these four principals in the Barbara Graham story were still in the natural order of things. But in January, 1958, it began to strike those whom Bloody Babs had specifically singled out for her retribution.

On January 22nd the Dutch freighter Bonita, steaming up the Mississippi channel in a fog south of New Orleans, rammed a converted shrimp boat and cut it in two. One man was saved as the shrimp boat sank, but the other four aboard, all professional divers on their way to a salvage operation in the Gulf of Mexico, were drowned. Among them was John True, then aged 42, the man who had wriggled out of a murder rap by testifying against his accomplices.

A few days later, on January 28th, Judge Fricke, who had passed the death sentence on the trio, succumbed to cancer at the age of 75. Barbara's lawyer had mockingly called the judge "the 13th juror."

On the rainy night of February 19th, 1958, less than a month after John True took his last dive, podgy Bill Upshaw's time ran out with equal abruptness. Driving his Cadillac convertible at high speed along US Highway 99 in the desert near Indio, he pulled out to overtake a bus. He failed to note that the road narrowed at this point for a bridge over a canal. Before he could swing back in time his car hit the bus. He and his companions were killed instantly in the splintering crash.

That wound up the death roster on the infamous mob. Bloody Babs could at last rest easy in her grave.

But not for long, perhaps. Soon her grim story was resurrected and blazoned all over the world with the release of the movie sensation *I Want To Live*, in which Susan Hayward won an Oscar for her portrayal of the convicted and executed murderess. The trouble was that the screenplay, while claiming to be "based on the actual facts," took artistic liberties with them. It left the strong implication that the state of California had railroaded an innocent woman to the gas chamber, apparently because she had a dubious past, and because she had refused to co-operate with the police.

The film, seen by thousands of people who had never heard of the Mabel Monahan case before, stirred worldwide controversy over capital punishment. The anti-death-penalty lobby hailed it as a classic documentary exposing the "tragic futility" of judicial murder. California lawmen, on the other hand, condemned the picture, branding it as distorted.

Deputy District Attorney Miller Leavy, who had prosecuted the Monahan case, called the movie "a black mark on the Californian justice administration." He blasted the film's contention the Barbara was left-handed, while Mrs. Monahan had been pistol-whipped by a right-handed person. He produced jail records that proved Barbara was right-handed.

It was also pointed out that the picture was confined entirely to Barbara's involvement in the Monahan case, while lightly skipping over the Santo mob's gory background of mass murder.

The furore over the film had barely died down when the Barbara Graham case was revived on the emotional impetus of the worldwide clamour generated over the pending execution of another condemned Californian criminal, Caryl Chessman. The ghost of Bloody Babs walked once again in March, 1960, when Deputy DA Leavy was called to testify before a state senate committee discussing a bill for the abolition of capital punishment. The bill was drafted by Governor Edmund Brown, who had just given the latest stay of execution to Chessman.

Leavy came up with the startling revelation that Barbara had confessed her guilt to the former San Quentin Warden Teets after her transfer from Corona Prison. Leavy said he had been told this in June, 1959, by another lawyer, named William Weissich, to whom Teets confided the information only two days before his sudden death in 1957. Teets told Weissich that he could see no reason to make the confession public, since Bloody Babs had already been convicted. The lawyer had considered the information confidential.

Weissich later told newsmen that Teets had indeed told him of Barbara's confession. Another lawyer, Louis Nelson, then revealed that Teets had told him the same thing. When Nelson told Teets that he was still haunted by a gruesome Death Row confession made to him by another prisoner, Teets said: "I know how you feel about it. It's part of the job. I had to listen to Barbara Graham telling me how she pistol-whipped Mrs. Monahan and split her head open. It's a load I've been carrying for a long time."

Some time after the warden's death Nelson and Weissich discussed the matter and decided not to tell anyone, since revelation would serve no purpose. Weissich later passed the information to Leavy. Asked why he hadn't spoken about it before, Leavy said he was waiting for an opportune occasion. By the time he received the information, he said, the film had already "done its damage" to the cause of law enforcement.

The last footnote to the bloody story of Barbara Graham was written on June 2nd, 1960, when Mrs. Olivia Shorter filed a legal petition to have her husband Baxter declared legally dead. The necessary seven years having elapsed, the petition was granted on June 21st, enabling her to receive money from the sale of their house. Thus the grim total of the Santo mob's killings was brought officially to seven.

3 – HORROR OF THE LAST WALK
Ruth Snyder

Magazine art editor Albert Snyder was having a bad day. When a misdirected phone call was put through to his office by mistake he blew a fuse.

The phone operator, Ruth Brown, metaphorically staggered back under Snyder's wrath. "Sorry! Sorry!" she said helplessly. "But everyone makes a mistake just once in a while. Maybe even you!" With that, she broke the connection.

Ten minutes later Snyder rang her back. He was full of contrition, overflowing with apologies. "Please come out to dinner with me tonight," he pleaded. "I want to apologise in person."

Ruth sniffed. "Don't worry," she said. "It isn't that important."

"Please!" Snyder insisted. "I'm looking for a new assistant anyway, and you have the sort of voice I'm looking for."

It sounded like a ploy as old as creation, but as it happened Ruth was fed up with her job. She was 19, and a bit of adventure, she decided, wouldn't go amiss either. She agreed the date, wore a low-cut dress, and enjoyed watching his eyes bulge with admiration as she casually leaned forward over the dinner table.

Snyder, a 32-year-old bachelor, was hooked that night. From then on he took her out to dance halls, theatres, restaurants, nightclubs – wherever there was fun to be had and the day's work could be forgotten. He gave her an engagement ring for Christmas, 1914, and they were married the following July.

And that, it seems, was the end of the romance.

For as soon as the knot was tied Albert called for his slippers, sat down in his favourite chair at the fireside, and nodded off. It was at this point that Ruth realised just how hopelessly mismatched they were. She had signed up for a life that her carefree heart had no desire for.

In November, 1917, she gave birth to a daughter,

Lorraine. This event failed to heal the breach widening in her marriage. Albert especially was soon fed up with being a father, resenting the disturbance to his sleep.

His only consolation was that he moved up in the world. They bought a house on Long Island, New York, and Ruth's mother Josephine moved in to help with Lorraine. With Albert away at work in Manhattan for 10 hours a day and her child well cared for, Ruth had time on her hands to indulge herself with her pleasure-seeking friends.

In July, 1925, she was dining with some of them in a Manhattan restaurant when she was introduced to a newcomer, Judd Gray. He was a shy, weak personality – just the type that Ruth liked to dominate. He told her that his wife was a respectable, virtuous woman with no interest in her life except caring for their daughter.

"What do you do for a living?" Ruth asked.

"I'm a travelling salesman in ladies' underwear," Judd replied.

The following month, while Albert was away, Judd rang and invited her for dinner. At the end of it she had accepted his instant invitation to buy her a corset from his firm, the Bien Jolie Corset Company on Fifth Avenue. It was nearly midnight when he let her into the showroom. He took her measurements as delicately as possible, and then told her to sit down while he went off to get a stock of appropriate corsets.

When he returned a few minutes later Ruth had prepared herself for the fitting. She had taken off all her clothes and was standing before him completely naked.

Judd dropped his armful of corsets and wrapped his arms around her. "Just a minute," she said. She went to a clothes rack, picked up a couple of expensive fur coats and threw them on the floor as a makeshift bed. After that, the night passed speedily away.

For the next 18 months they conducted an affair of high passion, frequently at the Waldorf-Astoria hotel, Judd's stopover for nights when he was on business trips. They were an ideal couple. Judd's wife had long since given up the physical side of marriage, and Albert

Snyder had become cold and unemotional, incapable of satisfying Ruth's wild sexual caprices.

As their passion deepened, Ruth was the one who was in complete charge of the affair. She played on Judd's weakness by continually complaining about Albert. "He beats me, humiliates me, " she said. "He's so cruel to me." Then, turning to Judd with a tear in her eye, she said softly: "How wonderful life would be for us if only we were both free."

It says much for their relationship that the unfortunate lingerie salesman was so weak in her hands that he took to calling her "Mommie."

She had known him for only three months when she began talking about them both being free to marry each other, and undoubtedly murder was already in the frame, deep in the recesses of her mind. In November, 1925, she persuaded Albert to take out three insurances on his life. She paid the first premiums without his knowledge and instructed the postman to deliver all insurance letters to her personally. She stood to gain $96,000 if Albert died violently or in an accident.

One evening at the Waldorf-Astoria she told Judd: "I'm going to get rid of Albert."

Judd looked at her in horror. "You ought to see a doctor," he replied.

"I've already made four attempts," she went on. "Once I gave him a drink of drugged whisky while he was working on the car, and then closed the garage doors while the engine was running. But it didn't work."

Another time she left the gas on while Albert was asleep on a settee in the living-room. Then she tried to poison him with bichloride of mercury, and after that failed she tried to gas him while he slept.

Albert didn't seem to mind when in October, 1925, Ruth and Judd went off together for a 10-day holiday filled with passion. Every minute of the day Ruth reminded her lover that if they were unencumbered with Albert, life would be one long glorious idyll like this.

She added: "Once we have Albert's insurance money, you'll never need to work again."

She was open about her intentions now. She wanted his help to kill her husband.

"Albert's bought a gun," she said. "I think he may try to shoot me with it." Casually, she added: "Do you know how to handle a revolver?"

"No," Judd said.

"You could learn. You could shoot him for me, before he shoots me."

Judd said: "I've never shot a man in my life and I'm not going to start with murder."

"In that case I'll have to do it by myself," she said. "But couldn't you at least give me a few ideas?"

Judd was resolute. "I'm not getting involved in any plans like this. Why don't we just elope and live together somewhere else?"

Ruth fell silent. They could of course do just that, but that would be saying goodbye to $96,000. She didn't just want sex, she wanted the money too.

She tried a new tack. If he were so adamant that he wouldn't help her, she said, they would inevitably drift apart. That meant that the heady, sex-laced nights would be gone for good. Judd would have to seek solace in the arms of his frigid wife.

If murder wasn't on Judd's mind, the thought of losing his passionate redhead was something he couldn't begin to contemplate. She had transported him into another world, a place he'd only ever dreamed about. It was a world to which he was now completely in thrall.

Slowly, his resistance began to crumble. Yes, he would help her, but only with advice. In March, 1927, she persuaded him to go to lunch at her home to discuss the plan.

"I'll chloroform him first, so he'll feel no pain," she said "Then I'll hit him with a heavy instrument, like a hammer."

"What about a sash weight?" Judd suggested. "It's only a suggestion, mind you. I don't want anything to do with the actual murder."

But two days later he bought a bottle of chloroform in a New York chemist's shop. A few yards farther down the street he bought a sash weight in a hardware shop. He handed these purchases to Ruth.

The next time they met she told him: "I've been practising with he sash weight. It's too heavy for me to swing properly. You'll have to help me."

Judd replied: "I can't do it alone. If I must do it, you'll have to help me."

Ruth smiled triumphantly to herself. She had at last persuaded him to do the killing for her. All he wanted was for her to be his accomplice. Now all she had to do was sketch out a murder plan.

The date was fixed for March 7th, 1927. On that day Ruth's mother would be away on a private nursing job. Ruth would drug Albert and then light a lamp in her mother's room to indicate that all was well. That would be the signal for Judd, waiting outside, to enter the house and despatch Albert.

On the appointed day Judd was duly waiting outside the house at 9 p.m. He was very tottery – he had drunk a quarter of a bottle of rye whisky to bolster his courage. For two and a half hours he paced up and down the street, waiting for he lamp to appear at the window. In despair, Ruth slipped out of the house and whispered: "He's still awake. He's sleepy, but he's still conscious."

Standing in the cold, dark street, Judd shuddered. He had no idea what he was doing there. He was to say much later: "She got me in such a whirl that I didn't know where I was." Suddenly, his nerve dissolved in the acrid taste of the rye whisky. He hurried back to the train station, returned to New York City, and next day went off to Buffalo on a business appointment.

At all costs now he wanted to put the nightmare scenario behind him. But Ruth had other ideas.

While he was in Buffalo she sent him nine letters and a telegram. The new date for the killing, she told him, was March 19th. He must bring a length of rope. She would leave the side door unbolted, allowing him to enter the house and hide in her mother's room until Albert and Lorraine returned from a party. Her mother would be away. She would leave a packet of cigarettes on the kitchen table to indicate that everything had so far gone according to plan.

Like a man hypnotised, Judd arrived in Syracuse, New York State, on March 18th, and registered at the Hotel Onondaga. In the lobby he chanced upon an old friend – Haddon Gray, who shared his surname but was no relation. As they chatted over drinks Judd had an idea.

"I'm going to spend tomorrow night with a girl," he told his friend. "I'd be obliged if you could hang a 'Do Not Disturb' sign on my bedroom door and ruffle up the bedclothes to make it look as if they've been slept in. I don't want my wife to be suspicious, you see."

Haddon Gray readily agreed. What he wasn't told was that he was unwittingly fixing an alibi for a killer. What Judd probably didn't realise at the time was that he was setting up evidence that his crime was premeditated.

Next evening Judd put two strands of picture wire, a small bottle of chloroform, some cotton rags, a piece of cheesecloth, and a handkerchief into his briefcase and set off for New York. During the journey he found an Italian newspaper on a seat and put that into his briefcase too. Arriving at Grand Central Station, he bought a return ticket to Syracuse for the next morning's train. And for the next hour and a half he walked through the rain to the Snyder home in Queens, sipping from a whisky flask. He arrived just after midnight.

The side door was unbolted, as Ruth had arranged, and the cigarettes were on the kitchen table. But he had drunk so much whisky he had forgotten what the cigarettes were meant to indicate, and he waited for another 15 minutes in the kitchen before finally deciding to go upstairs to the room of Ruth's mother, next to the Snyders' bedroom. He lay on the bed, his head spinning from the whisky.

That evening Albert, Ruth and Lorraine were at a party given by friends living a few minutes' drive away. Ruth had decided not to drink – Albert had more than one too many and was heavily intoxicated when they left for their home.

Upstairs in the vacant bedroom, Judd heard their car

arrive and their footsteps on the stairs. Ruth slipped into the darkened bedroom where he was hiding and whispered, "Are you there, dear?" and when Judd replied, she said, "Wait quietly and I'll be back shortly."

Albert fell quickly into an alcohol-induced sleep. Ruth crept into the room with Judd. "I don't know whether I can go through with it," he whispered. "But I'll try." They sat on the bed side by side, until about 3 a.m. Then Ruth went into Albert's room, ascertained that he was fast asleep, and returned to Judd. "Now's the time," she said.

Judd put on rubber gloves and gripped the sash weight. Ruth had the chloroform, a coil of wire, the handkerchief and cotton rags. She held his hand and guided him into the bedroom where her husband lay sleeping. Judd raised the weight and brought it down hard towards Albert's head, but in his drunken state he missed completely, hitting the bed head instead. The noise woke Albert, who sat up, spotted the intruder and lashed out.

As Albert's hands closed around his assailant's throat, Judd called out, "Mommie, Mommie, for God's sake help me!"

Ruth picked up the sash weight and smashed it against her husband's head again and again until he was dead. Judd, fuelled by alcohol and panic, continued to straddle the body, squeezing Albert's throat with his right hand and covering his mouth with his left.

When at last he realised that the struggle was over, he got off he bed and watched Ruth tie her husband's hands and feet. "Remember, this is supposed to look like a burglary," she said. "We've got to ransack the house next."

They washed the blood off their hands in the bathroom and Ruth took his bloodstained shirt and her bloodstained nightdress and burned them in the cellar. She also hid the sash weight.

They went back to Albert's bedroom in order to disarrange it for the faked burglary but the sight of the body on the bed was almost too much for Ruth. "Is he dead?" she asked. "He's got to be dead. This has got to go through or I'm ruined."

She asked Judd to pull the picture wire tight around Albert's neck, but he couldn't do it. He went downstairs for another drink, and by the time he returned Ruth had tied the wire for him. Then his nerve finally shattered.

"I'm through with you!" he yelled. Ruth took no notice. She emptied Albert's wallet and stuffed the money contents into Judd's pockets. She asked him to take her jewellery, but he refused. "Hide it somewhere," he said. "They probably won't know anything about it."

Ruth said: "You'll have to knock me unconscious. That's what a burglar would do." Judd couldn't do that, however. He placed the Italian newspaper he had picked up on the train in a prominent position and left her lying, gagged and bound, on her mother's bed. Then he staggered down the stairs and out into the dawn rain.

Back in Syracuse he told his friend Haddon Gray a story that would only help to break him. "I was at my girl friend's house when two intruders broke in and murdered her husband. After they'd gone I bent over his body to see whether he was still alive, and got blood on my clothes."

Haddon Gray believed him, and helped him to destroy his bloodstained coat.

Meanwhile, Ruth stayed on the bed where he had left her until next 8 a.m., and then dragged herself to her daughter's bedroom and knocked on the door. Terrified, Lorraine ran to the house of a neighbour, Louis Mulhauser, for help.

Louis Mulhauser was certain that a burglar had murdered Albert Snyder. A few weeks ago he had told Ruth about a stranger prowling the neighbourhood and peering into her bedroom. "He must have broken in, been spotted by Albert and killed him in panic," he declared.

The police listened to his story in silence, but they were soon unconvinced. They talked at length to Ruth. "I heard footsteps in the hall soon after I went to bed," she babbled. "I got up to investigate and saw two of them. They were dark and foreign-looking and had moustaches." Drawing attention to the Italian newspaper found in her mother's room, she ranted on, "It seemed to me they spoke Italian. They grabbed me and threw me on the bed. I felt a blow on my head and must have fainted away. I don't know what else happened until I spotted two of them."

The police surgeon shook his head when he heard her story. "If she really had received a blow heavy enough to knock her unconscious for several hours, she would have a bruise to show for it," he said. "I have no doubts she's lying, and she knows I think so. I told her I thought her story was ridiculous. She must know who killed her husband."

Detectives had no reason to doubt the doctor. Looking around the house they decided that what it all added up to was a thoroughly botched murder. There were no signs of forced entry, and the sash weight, heavily bloodstained, was soon discovered in the basement.

Ruth had been tied much too loosely for this to be the work of professionals, and the jewels she claimed to have been stolen were found under the mattress. Despite the ransacking, nothing seemed to have been taken. Even the bloodstained pillowcase had been deposited in the used linen basket.

Perhaps most damning of all, she hadn't called on Albert for help, but instead had let Lorraine seek the assistance of neighbours. The only reason for that must be that she knew her husband was already dead.

The great lie was further eroded as she was driven in custody to police headquarters. She asked Detective Jimmy Smith, who escorted her: "Doesn't my story sound convincing?"

When he told her it didn't, and the reasons why, she replied naively: "I can't help it if the burglars hid my jewels under the mattress. They must have done that to cause me trouble."

Hours later, after her interrogation at headquarters, she suddenly asked Detective Smith: "What do you think they'll give me if I talk? A couple of years?"

Smith hardly felt so, but didn't elaborate. Knowing that several love letters had been found in the house, addressed to "Momsie," he said: "Was he the man who helped you?"

She nodded. She took a handkerchief from her handbag and began to cry. Smith noted that this time, for the first time, they were real tears.

Her 50-page confession was slightly different from the version that Judd would give some time later. She said: "Judd walked into my husband's room. I stood in the hall. I saw him tie my husband's hands behind his back. I saw him use the chloroform. When he hit Al with the sash weight I put my hands over my ears. I walked away from the door. A little later Judd came out of the bedroom and said, 'I reckon that's it.'

"We hid the jewels. Judd wanted to take them with him, but I wouldn't trust him. Then he went away. I tied myself up and sent little Lorraine out to get help."

An hour later Syracuse Police arrested Judd Gray at the Hotel Onondaga. But they told New York Police on the phone: "You won't get far with him. He's got a cast-iron alibi. He can prove that he was in the hotel at 6.30 on Saturday night. The train from here to New York leaves at 5.30, so he couldn't have been in Queens at the time of the murder."

Even so, he was escorted back to New York by Police Inspector Liam Gallagher, and on the journey freely admitted his affair with Ruth. But as for killing her husband, "That's a ridiculous story. I'm a married man. I couldn't possibly have supported Ruth and my own family. Anyway, I have an alibi."

"I'm afraid your alibi has just fallen down," Gallagher announced. "We found a ticket stub for the 5.30 train Saturday evening, Syracuse to New York, in your hotel wastepaper basket. The chambermaid, it seems, failed to empty the wastepaper basket on Sunday morning." So saying, he produced the ticket stub.

Now it was Judd's turn to confess. He insisted that the murder had been Ruth's idea. "She hounded me into killing him. She drove me crazy. She committed the murder despite my protests. She administered the chloroform, used the picture wire and hit her husband over the head with the sash weight."

His alibi was faked with the help of his friend Haddon Gray. He had asked Gray to stay in the room, make phone calls and post letters, to give everyone the impression he was still there.

The trial of Ruth Snyder and Judd Gray began on April 18th, 1927, and proved to be a worldwide sensation. Ruth emerged as an icy, ruthless, and scheming woman, with no apparent regret for what she had done. They called her the Iron Widow, while Judd was dubbed the Putty Man. He was much more kindly received by the public.

Occasionally during the trial Ruth broke down and wept, a performance that bought laughter and jeers from the audience. Even so, she received more than 160 proposals of marriage from admirers.

The jury found the lovers guilty in less than two hours. They were sentenced to die in the electric chair on January 12th, 1928.

There were no good reasons for a reprieve or for a new trial, but at first Ruth convinced herself that they wouldn't execute her. She paced the death cell at Sing Sing expecting every day to hear news of a reprieve. When it didn't come, she called a priest and converted to the Roman Catholic faith.

She was a model prisoner on Death Row. The prison's assistant matron, Lillian Hickey, remembered in a magazine article: "I grew quite fond of her. She was never querulous, never inclined to argue, never impatient or restless. She would describe her crime at length, but never admit her guilt, and I pretended to believe her innocence. She had delightful little mannerisms and bursts of generosity. She was one of the most amiable and attractive young women I have ever known."

Mrs. Hickey had high praise for Ruth's courage, too. She said: "From the moment she entered the death house to the last, till the moment when the lethal switch was thrown, she never exhibited the slightest fear of her certain and ignominious death."

When Christmas 1927 approached, Ruth, it seemed, had adopted a fatalistic approach. According to Mrs. Hickey, she would say, "I've got to die some time, so why not now?"

The assistant matron recalled: "Very often she would sing in that sweet, rich voice of hers and I often thought she was singing to Judd, for her clear notes would have carried easily to his cell. The song she usually sang was some popular theme to which, she told me, she and her lover had often danced in the days before the murder.

"She once told me, 'The happiest days of my life were those I spent with Judd.'"

On the day of her execution, Ruth had a bowl of cereal, some toast and a cup of coffee for breakfast. She still believed there might be a stay of execution. But Death Row inmates who were about to be executed were always ordered to take a hot shower bath. It was Mrs Hickey's job to tell Ruth that she must now have a hot bath.

"She began to cry quietly, without hysteria. All during her bath, she cried softly. Later that morning her mother and brother came and guards placed a mesh screen between Ruth and her visitors. Ruth objected to this customary procedure. 'I can't see why I can't kiss my mother goodbye. There's no harm in that.'"

To spare her pain, officials decided to tell her nothing in advance, and because the prison doctor thought it might make her hysterical they did not ask her what she wanted for her last meal. Instead she was presented with a chicken dinner.

When she finished eating she played cards with Mrs. Hickey and another matron. At 10.30 that night she was taken from her cell to a cell adjoining the death chamber. Mrs. Hickey said she took this last walk "chatting casually. Approaching death failed utterly to move her."

Mrs. Hickey's recall may, however, have been dressed up for her magazine audience, for other reports claim that Ruth was fearful to the point of hysteria. According to one account she told a guard at 5 p.m. on the execution day, "I've been reprieved. Or at least I have a stay of execution."

The guard, who knew better, asked her why she thought so. "Because it's almost supper time, and the warden hasn't been here to ask me what I want to eat," she replied triumphantly. "If I were to be executed I'd have my choice of menu."

When the time came to move her to the cell next to the death chamber, and she realised what it meant. she burst into a fit of sobbing. "No!' she cried. "No! No! I'm too young to die. You can't kill me. And what about my baby? Who's going to look after my baby?" When, later, she was told there was no hope, she wept uncontrollably.

With a trembling hand she asked to write a last message. It read: "I am very, very sorry I have sinned and I am paying dearly for it. I can only hope that my life – that I am giving up now – will serve as a lesson to the world."

The custom with double executions was to execute the less brave of the two first. There was no doubt that Judd Gray was putting up a stoical front. Ruth, it was decided, must die first.

There were 28 witnesses, including reporters who were warned not to take photographs. When the door was opened to admit Ruth, three chaplains, two Roman Catholic and one Protestant, preceded her. She was alongside Mrs. Hickey and another matron. She was dressed a rough grey cotton smock, the death shroud. She appeared shrunken. As she sat in the electric chair the two matrons wept.

Suddenly she shrieked: "Oh, Father, forgive them for they know not what they do!"

As one of the Catholic priests stood before her with a crucifix held high, she cried out: "Father, forgive me! Oh, Father, forgive me!"

Seconds later she shrieked again: "Father, forgive them! Father, oh Father, forgive them!" and broke into a fit of hysteria.

Fingers trembling, executioner Robert Elliott adjusted the head cap. As the death mask dropped over her face, her lips moved in desperate prayer. Elliott strode towards the switch and threw it.

Ruth's legs strained against the leg bar. Her arms wrenched stiff against their fastenings Her chest rose and fell.

A photographer in the audience had a hidden camera strapped to his leg. As Ruth's twisting body lurched against the straps he took the famous photograph of her dying.

For a minute or two longer the electric current sapped all the life out of Ruth's body. At a signal from the prison warden, Elliott threw off the switch and two doctors examined the body.

The remains of Ruth Snyder, with gaping mouth and protruding tongue, were carried away on a steel stretcher to an adjoining room for a post-mortem.

Five minutes later Judd Gray was escorted through the door. He wore black trousers and a white shirt. He sat in the electric chair, said nothing, and stared fixedly ahead He took less than a minute to die, then his body too was carried into the post-mortem room. The bodies of the two lovers were placed side by side on white tables.

Now, at least, they were together for eternity.

4 – "WHAT WILL HAPPEN TO MY CHILDREN?"
Anna Antonio

To a casual observer it would have looked harmless enough. They were three Italians having a night out. Two had somehow managed to remain sober, but they were pre-occupied with their friend, Salvatore Antonio, who had drunk too much.

There were no casual observers, though. The three men had stopped their car on a lonely section of the road a few miles south of Albany, in New York State. Salvatore wanted to be sick.

He got out of the car and staggered to the side of the road, where he raised a hand to lean against a tree. One of his companions walked over to him. The darkness obscured the gun in his hand. The third man emerged from the car and stood by the front bumper, the darkness concealing the hunting knife he was holding.

The man with the gun fired five times. The drunken Antonio slumped to the ground, but astonishingly, he was still alive.

"Help me!" he begged. "Help me! You are my friends. Why are you doing this to me?"

"I can't help you," the man with the gun said. "I must go through with this."

The other man came forward and swung his knife in swift, downward strokes, stabbing Antonio 14 times. Then the assassins sped away in their car, leaving their victim crumpled on the road.

An hour later another car came by. The two men in it picked up Antonio and drove him to hospital in Albany, where he died on the operating table.

After that, murder squad detectives moved into high gear. They spoke first to Anna Antonio, the victim's wife, who tearfully disclosed her suspicions that her husband had been trafficking in narcotics and that he might also have been part of an arson ring.

"They took him for a ride," she wept. "I warned him that something like this might happen, but he only laughed at me."

She had three children, but it hadn't exactly been a marriage made in heaven. Antonio was a labourer, a poor provider, and Anna was sick of the drudgery. They quarrelled furiously. Neighbours had even heard her screaming at her husband once, "I hope you die!"

Detectives trawled through Antonio's friends and settled on two – Samuel Feraci and Vincent Saetta. What interested the investigators about them was that they had invited Antonio for a car ride on the evening of Easter Sunday 1932 – the same evening that Antonio was savagely murdered.

Feraci and Saetta spent many hours in custody denying all knowledge of the murder. When they finally broke down Feraci claimed that Anna, the victim's wife, had orchestrated the plot. He claimed that she talked him into it by promising to pay him $800 for the killing.

Thinking that he couldn't pull it off alone, he enlisted Saetta's help, promising him $200. He gave Saetta an advance of $75, with the balance to be paid when Anna collected the $5,300 insurance.

Anna Antonio was promptly arrested. She, too, initially denied everything. She only gave in when detectives confronted her with a taxi driver who had driven her to Feraci's home a few hours after the murder. She screamed: "All right, all right! I'll tell you all about it!"

On April 15th, 1933, a jury listened to the story of what happened as Anna stood in the dock with Feraci and Saetta. "We took Antonio for a good ride towards Hudson," Saetta said. "I brought a gun. Feraci had a knife. I pulled my gun. I fired the shots."

Feraci said: "I hear bang, bang, bang! Then Saetta runs round the car and points to the knife. Antonio was lying in the road. He said to me, 'Sam, please, I never did anything to you.' I said I can't help it. I got to do it. So I did the stabbing."

The trio of killers were taken to Sing Sing's Death Row. When they had been there 13 months Anna's final appeal was turned down and her execution was set for June 24th, 1934. But few thought seriously that she would go to the chair, for, it was argued, who could possibly execute the mother of three children?

The three children were indeed vital to her chance of survival. When she won a clemency hearing before the state governor at his mansion in Albany she took the children with her. He lawyer pleaded: "Must these little ones suffer so?" The governor, who was privately opposed to capital punishment, said he would give his decision later.

He did. In his judgement he said he had no choice under the law but to allow the sentence to stand.

Up to this point Anna had wept constantly, frequently breaking into hysterics. Now she was calm. She told her lawyer: "I know I'm going to die. I don't mind. There never was any real hope." Before the lawyer left she wrote out her will, bequeathing her few meagre possessions to her children.

On the morning of June 28th she awoke from an all but sleepless night. She put on a pink cotton dress with a white collar, and then picked at the food on her breakfast tray, with no appetite. "I'm ill and heartbroken," she said. "There is so much to live for, and I will not live. Only a few months ago I was young. Now, very soon, I will die. What have I done?"

The suspense had taken a heavy toll on her looks. Dark shadows were etched under her large, luminous brown eyes, and her shapeless figure had lost its roundness. She was only 28, but she looked 40. Her long, wavy hair had once been her great pride. She used to brush the tresses vigorously, pinning them up to form an elaborate frame for her round, pretty, dimpled face. Now her hair was stringy, and felt coarse under her fingers.

The grey day dragged on into evening. By 6 p.m. all preparations for the triple execution were completed. The executioner had arrived and taken up his post in the chamber where, before that night was over, he would earn $450 – $150 for each of the condemned upon whom he would carry out the law's sentence. Up the hilly road from Ossining, small groups of people walked quietly towards the prison gates, where they gathered in clusters to maintain a death vigil.

Anna's last visitor from outside was her brother. He left the prison a 9 p.m. and told reporters that his doomed sister had eaten nothing. "She didn't even give an order for a meal. She couldn't eat … She is so brave. She prays, but she is not afraid to die. She made me kneel down with her and pray. She gave me the gold cross from around her neck and told me to give it to her boy. I told her I would do that."

The principal reason why authority had set itself against intervention was that it would have seemed unfair to reprieve Anna but to allow the two assassins to die. If it were only Anna's life at stake, perhaps clemency would have been shown.

Saetta and Feraci were housed close to her cell. But none of the trio could see one another and no words were exchanged between them

Anna was now transferred to the pre-execution cell. A barber came in and shaved a circle two or three inches in diameter on the top of her skull. It was on this bald spot that the electrode of the death helmet would make contact. Anna stared straight in front of her. "My children, my children!" she muttered. "What will they do now? I hope they won't judge me too harshly. I hope they will be happy. I hope… I hope …"

The last hour began. At 10.10, with just 50 minutes to go, came drama.

"I have to see the warden at once," Vincent Saetta told a guard. The warden was summoned to the death house.

"I m totally responsible for the murder," Saetta told him. "Antonio and me, we had a quarrel over money. As a matter of fact, he owed me $75 and refused to pay. I decided to kill him. Mrs. Antonio had no knowledge of my intention. She is absolutely innocent of this crime."

The warden hurried off and phoned the state governor. At 11.25, the warden entered the room where the official witnesses were waiting impatiently. "I have only this much to say," he said in the hush that greeted his arrival. "I have been in touch with the governor."

Was there to be a reprieve, everyone wanted to know?

The warden replied: "I cannot say at this time." He turned on his heel and left the room.

Anna seemed not to have noticed that it was now past the time of her execution. She was in a trance.

At 1.14 a.m. the warden returned to the room of waiting witnesses, and everyone clamoured to question him. He stood in impassive silence until they calmed down, and then said, "The state governor has directed me to postpone the three executions for 24 hours while he studies and considers a long statement made by Vincent Saetta just before 11 p.m. tonight."

Anna was not told of the reprieve until 3.15 a.m. She had collapsed in a faint at 1 a.m.

So she lived another day on borrowed time, living in a trance, refusing food, oblivious to everything around her. Her lawyer appealed to the state governor for time to ask for a new trial, but the district attorney said: "Saetta's statement is absolute lies."

Judge Earl Gallup rejected the appeal for a new trial but Anna was granted another reprieve to give her attorney time to make yet another move on her behalf. Told by the matron that this had happened, she exclaimed: "Thank God! I still live. I still have time to see my children again."

In the event, it was all a false dawn. On August 8th the Supreme Court in Albany denied another request for a new trial. "I m painfully aware of the gravity of my decision," said the judge.

When Anna was informed that this, her third reprieve, had been denied, she stared at the matron in disbelief, a cold fist of horror clutching at her heart. She had been so confident. She turned to her bed and sank to the floor beside it. Her lips moved in prayer, her shoulders shook with sobs that racked her whole body.

The ordeal was clearly exhausting her. She hadn't eaten anything for several days, only sipping at coffee. He weight had fallen to six stone.

The execution was now fixed for August 12th, which was the seventh birthday of her daughter Marie. At Sing Sing executions were always on a Thursday and on

Wednesday night she was given sedatives in the hope that she would sleep. Instead she spent the long night sitting upright on her bed, staring blankly at the wall. Occasionally her eyes would droop and she would be on the point of drowsing; then she would come fully awake with a start and continue to stare at the wall.

At 8 a.m. a matron brought in her breakfast. Anna refused to touch the food, and just sipped the coffee. When she was asked what she would like for her last meal she didn't reply. Finally she muttered: "God alone can help me. I'm not thinking of myself so much. I'm thinking of what it will mean to the future of my children. Nobody can know how terrible it is to be here except someone who has gone through it."

Occasionally she sobbed hysterically, and sometimes she uttered a piercing scream.

In the afternoon she was persuaded to come out of her cell for a while and sit in the corridor, where she could hear the radio playing. She listened to a comedy sketch and a musical programme. Suddenly the music was interrupted. An announcer said: "Latest flash from Albany! The governor has refused a further reprieve for Mrs. Antonio. She must die in the electric chair tonight." A matron switched off the radio too late. Anna, her eyes wild, shouted: "They have all deserted me!"

She refused last visits from her brother and his wife and a nephew, and agreed to see only her youngest child, Frankie, aged three. She took the small boy into her arms, caressed him, wept over him. "I'm going away," she said. "I'm going away for a long time." Her last words to him were, "I hope you grow up to be a good man, Frankie."

Her brother took the boy away and returned alone at 7 p.m. He found her in quite a different mood.

"Let's make believe it isn't going to happen," she said. "Let's pretend I'll still be here tomorrow, and the next day and the next. Let's look forward to your visit with me the next time. There isn't going to be any end. Just try to remember that. No end at all. I shall be here the next time you call."

The brother stared at his sister, to whom he had been virtually father and mother since their parents died 21 years ago. She seemed serene, subdued, resigned. But her cheeks were sunken and her eyes lacked sparkle. Her body was skin and bones, her hair in disarray.

"Don't say goodbye," she repeated. "Remember the good times."

"I'll see you tomorrow," he said, forcing a smile.

Now it was time for the barber to come back. There have been instances when prisoners were so irrational by the time the barber came to trim them that they mistook the barber's chair for the electric chair, and the barber for the executioner. When he arrived in the death cell, Anna turned to the matron who was ever present and said, "It's going to be, I guess." After he'd gone she put on the dress in which she was going to die – a blue dress, with blue trimmings, which she had made in her cell. One of the matrons had freshly washed, starched and ironed it for her.

She went on talking for several minutes, rambling, almost incoherent. Scattered in among her muttered musings were bits of recollected information about her crime. She said one of the co-defendants had told her he was going to kill her husband, and she had replied, "I don't care what you do." As for killing him herself, she said that she could have done it easily at any time, "for there were always plenty of guns and dope in the house to do it with."

That was as close as she ever came to confessing her part in the murder.

A few minutes later she was kneeling and praying alongside a priest. At 11 p.m. the guards came for her. The priest asked, "Are you ready, my child?"

Anna nodded. She got to her feet and took a long look around her cell. She studied the picture of her children, picked it up and kissed it.

The principal keeper led the way from the women's wing through the central corridor lined by the cells of the condemned men. Anna walked firmly, responding to the prayers of the priest at her side. Two matrons walked behind in case she faltered. But they weren't needed.

The "last mile" took her past the cells of Saetta and Feraci, but she didn't give them so much as a glance. She walked one hundred paces before she reached the door of the death chamber. It opened on a room flooded with bright light. The eyes of the witnesses stared at her. She saw the chair, and just as the principal keeper motioned to her, she stepped forward quickly. She paused in front of the chair, and then sat down.

The matrons came forward to fasten the strap around her chest. They held her thin white arms while the male guards tightened the other straps. She continued to pray even after the hood was placed over her head, and the room was so still that her soft voice filled it.

The two matrons, with a guard between them, stood in front of the chair, not more than four feet away, blocking the view of the witnesses. Only these three, two women and one man, actually saw her die.

An official gave the signal by dropping his arm. The executioner pulled the switch. The current coursed through Anna's body. The executioner manipulated his controls for a second, and then there was a third shock of electricity.

The prison doctor stepped forward, placed a stethoscope against Anna's chest, and stepped back. "I pronounce this woman dead," he said.

It was 11.17 p.m. on August 12th, 1934. During the next 15 minutes Feraci and Saetta followed Anna in death.

Just after her death Governor Herbert Lehman issued a statement. It said: "The case has received my most painstaking and careful consideration from the time the Court of Appeals affirmed the conviction of Mrs. Antonio and her co-defendants.

"The responsibility of carrying out the death penalty on a woman is so distressing that frankly I sought to find any fact which would justify my interference with the course of justice. I have studied the record with the greatest of care. I reprieved all three defendants so that the case of Anna Antonio could again be submitted and considered in the courts of the state.

"I have no found any circumstances which would, under my oath of office and the duty I owe to all of the people of the state, justify the commuting of her sentence. I am certain that ... there are very few instances where the case of any person tried for murder in the first degree has been given greater study and examination.

"In the case of Mrs. Antonio the trial jury found her guilty. The Court of Appeals unanimously affirmed that verdict. Motions for a new trial, on newly discovered evidence, were made in the County Court and in the Supreme Court. Both were denied. The Court of Appeals has also denied an appeal and a motion for a re-argument.

"I am convinced that each of the three defendants is guilty. Appeals have been made to me to grant executive clemency to Anna Antonio on account of her sex, but the law makes no distinction of sex in the punishment of crime; nor would my own conscience or the duty imposed upon me by my oath of office permit me to do so. Each of the defendants is guilty. The crime and the manner of its execution are abhorrent. I have found no just and sound reason for the exercise of executive clemency.

"The administration of justice must be definite and certain, so that society may be protected and respect and observance of the law maintained."

An odd feature of Anna's time on Death Row was the comparatively large sum of money the state spent keeping her there. The bill for her sojourn in the death house was $4,650 – making her the most expensive Death Row inmate ever at Sing Sing up until that time.

There was no shortage of women volunteers willing to guard her while she was on Death Row. When she was first sentenced to death there were a number of applications from substantial housewives in nearby Ossining for one of the three positions as matron. One of the attractions undoubtedly was that the pay was unusually good.

5 – THE TRIGGER-HAPPY WAITRESS
Irene Schroeder

When she was only 16 years old Irene Crawford married rather hastily. She spent the next five years in leisurely repentance.

This was not really the fault of husband Don Schroeder. He was in fact a young man of an unusually high percentage of husbandly virtues. He was serious, hardworking and ambitious. For his first – and as it turned out his last – matrimonial home he rented and furnished a modern apartment in Wheeling, West Virginia, and toiled diligently to maintain it, and to provide for his wife and his son Donnie, who was born in 1924.

Irene was a pretty girl. She had blonde hair; her complexion was fair and her skin as soft as her heart and mind were hard. She was vain and domineering, and as strong-willed as reinforced concrete.

She also had a thirst for excitement and a desire for what she called good times. But these things required more money than her harassed husband was able to earn, and this led to arguments. It also led to Irene's protracted absences from home, during which she systematically performed some serious violations of the Seventh Commandment.

While having these good times she met Glenn Dague, a married man with two children and an unblemished reputation – at least until he met Irene. He was an insurance man, a Sunday school teacher and an active worker in the Boy Scout movement.

Shortly after meeting Irene, Dague voluntarily exchanged all these virtuous assets for the passionate embraces of the blonde who one day was to accompany him to the death chamber.

Dague fell desperately in love with Irene. It seems that she felt the same way about him. With one eye on her new lover, she divorced her young husband and took a job as a waitress in a restaurant.

Dague didn't bother about getting a divorce for himself. He simply left his wife and children to fend for themselves as best they could, then moved into a cheap hotel near the restaurant where Irene worked. Word soon got around and he was dismissed from his Sunday school job and asked to resign from the Boy Scout movement. Within a month the insurance firm for which he worked also decided to dispense with his services. He was sacked – for these were times when employers still took a moralistic attitude to their employees' behaviour.

Irene got what she wanted and she should have been happy. She was no longer married to a man she didn't particularly like, she was independent, she had found a lover, yet her life remained almost as dull as it had been before.

Most of the problem was about money. Her earnings as a waitress were meagre, and now Glenn was out of work. This wasn't the right formula for someone who always dreamed of living high on the vine. She thought about the problem and then came up with a solution that left Glenn Dague gasping.

"Honey," she said, "we're living like hillbillies. We were made for better things."

Dague agreed with that, and immediately put his finger on the crux of the matter. "We need money," he said. "But I guess I can't figure out any way to get it."

"I can," Irene replied. "I've got it all worked out. We'll get a car. We'll travel all over the country, stopping at the best hotels, eating in the best restaurants. We don't want to stay here all our lives. As we drive around, we'll pick up the cash as we need it."

Dague, who wasn't the brain of West Virginia, looked puzzled. "Where?" he asked. "How?"

"Oh, service stations, stores, places like that. We just hold them up. It'll be easy."

Glenn Dague had deserted his family, lost his job and dedicated himself to illicit love. But a small area of his conscience remained.

"We can't do that," he said. "First, it's wrong. Second, we'll get caught." He shook his head. "The first man we hold up is bound to call the police. Then we'll both be put in the slammer."

"Not if he's looking into the business end of a revolver, he won't," Irene declared.

Dague blinked stupidly. "You mean we're going to carry guns?"

She looked at her lover with a trace of contempt. "Did you ever hear of a hold-up artist who didn't carry a gun? Do you think a guy will hand over his money because he just likes the look of our sweet little faces? Of course we'll carry guns. What's more, we'll use them if we have to."

Dague shook his head. This decidedly wasn't for him. He wanted no part of it, he declared. But women have a way with men like Dague, and Irene had a special way. Very soon her iron will and her complaisant body were working miracles on his conscience. They changed his mind and he agreed to join his mistress in their new career.

They would not work entirely alone, Irene decided. She enlisted the help of her brother, Tom Crawford, who already had a minor criminal record.

In August, 1929, the trio were ready for action. Irene bought a Buick, which she registered in her father's name. Somehow or other she acquired three guns, and at the last minute she decided sentimentally that she could not embark on the trip without her five-year-old son Donnie.

She picked up the boy at her father's home, where he was staying, loaded him into the rear seat of the Buick with Tom Crawford, got into the front and, with Glenn Dague at the wheel, they set out.

They drove first into Ohio where they pulled their first job on September 1st, holding up the Meadowlark Inn on the outskirts of Cadiz. They were astonished just how simple it was. Like taking candy from kids, Irene reflected jubilantly.

Tom Crawford stayed in the car with young Donnie while Irene and Dague advanced menacingly on the inn's proprietor, William Willett. Each carried a gun. It was Irene who took the cash from Willett's pocket and relieved the cash register of the day's takings. The getaway was clean and fast.

The threesome celebrated on their booty for three days before heading back to West Virginia. Late in the afternoon of September 5th, 1929, the Buick rolled down the Waynesburg turnpike and through the town of Moundsville. It pulled up outside Jack Cotts' lunchroom and filling station some four miles out of town.

While they cased the place they bought pop and ice cream cones. Then they drove off, planning to return at midnight when, under cover of darkness, they would hold up the place.

Jack Cotts stared at the two menacing gun barrels and hastily co-operated. He handed over $30 from his own wallet and watched helplessly as they took $40 more from the cash register. The Buick was 30 miles away before the sheriff arrived in response to his call.

Glenn Dague, his strict moral compass thrown overboard, was now prepared to admit that Irene Schroeder had come up with a winner. Not only was this an easy business, it seemed to him less risky and much more enjoyable than selling insurance.

A week later Irene looked up from the newspaper she was reading and laughed out loud. Her brother and Dague looked across at her. "What's so funny?"

"I told you this would be a cinch," she chuckled. "Not only are we clean, but the sheriff's picked up a guy and his wife for that job we pulled in Moundsville. No one even suspects us. We should have been in this business a long time ago. We've been wasting our time working."

They certainly wasted no more time during that autumn of 1929. The black Buick, with its three adult criminals and an innocent boy, raced though West Virginia, Ohio and Pennsylvania. They held up a score of places, their levelled guns magically opening wallets and cash tills. Miraculously they escaped each time, evading roadblocks and police dragnets.

Christmas that year brought a brief lull in their rampage, but on Friday, December 27th, the Irene Schroeder mob carried out its most ambitious exploit. The Buick pulled up in front of Kroger's grocery store in

Butler, Pennsylvania. They left the engine running and little Donnie in the back seat as they bust in, covering the staff and customers with three revolvers.

It took only a couple of minutes to empty the till, and then the Buick was speeding off down the road towards New Castle. Still shaking with fear, the store manager called the state police.

Only a week previously, Governor John Fisher and Major Lynn Adams, head of the Pennsylvania state constabulary, had inaugurated a police teletype system connecting 95 cities and towns throughout the state. The Kroger's store hold-up was to be the first real test of its usefulness.

Officials in Lawrence County, among others, studied their teletyper as it spat out the message: a black car, containing a woman and two men suspected of an armed hold-up, was heading towards New Castle. Two highway patrolmen, Corporal Brady Paul and Private Ernest Moore, were despatched to Highway 422 to intercept the fugitive car.

A few minutes later the two patrolmen identified a car that seemed to answer the teletype description of the wanted vehicle as it roared down the road. Moore turned the police car round, blocking the highway, and the black car, a Buick, came to a shuddering stop. As Corporal Paul got out of the police car and approached the Buick, he saw a woman and a child in the back seat.

Over his shoulder he shouted back to Moore: "This can't be bandits. There's a kid in the car."

Paul approached the driver and asked to see his licence.

"Sure thing," said Tom Crawford. He opened the door, got out on to the road, and fumbled in his hip pocket as if seeking his wallet. He did not produce it. Instead he produced a revolver.

Paul had no chance to reach for his own weapon. He yelled to Moore: "Get your gun out! I'm covered! I –"

He never finished the sentence. For Irene Schroeder leaned out of the rear window of the Buick and fired twice. As Corporal Paul crumpled to the ground, she calmly turned her gun towards Moore and fired two more shots in his direction. Then she said, as serenely as if she were ordering groceries: "All right, Tom. Let's get out of here. And we'd better get another car. This one's hot."

"Where," Glenn asked, "can we get another car?"

"Anywhere, stupid!" Irene retorted. "Don't you know you can get anything with a gun?"

As Tom Crawford drove off at top speed, Dague peered out of the rear window at the two figures huddled in the road behind them. He closed his eyes and shuddered. Was this such a good idea after all, he wondered? It seemed that in the space of a couple of minutes the easy life had taken on a whole new dimension.

Nevertheless, Irene was about to prove her maxim again – "with a gun you can get anything." Speeding out of town, they overtook a car driven by Ray Horton, a New Castle businessman. With Irene rapping out the orders from the back seat, the Buick suddenly swerved to the right, blocking the road completely. Horton stamped on his brake and only just missed crashing into the Buick.

He stared in astonishment as a young blonde woman got out of he blocking vehicle. She pointed a gun at Horton. "Get out of that car and make it quick!" she yelled. Horton wasted no time in doing just as he was told.

"Come on, boys, let's go!" Irene shouted. Dague, carrying little Donnie, leapt into Horton's car followed by Irene, who still had her gun pointed at Horton. Tom Crawford drove the Buick ahead for a short distance before ditching it in a patch of woodland alongside the road. When he had rejoined the others they headed west in the hijacked car, while the unfortunate Horton trudged back to town on foot.

Back on Highway 422, Private Ernest Moore, unconscious from a bullet that had grazed his skull, was rushed to hospital. Tragically, for Corporal Paul there was no such need for haste. One of Irene's bullets had killed him instantly. The blonde hold-up woman had become a murderer.

Police in Pennsylvania, Ohio and West Virginia scrambled to search for the killers. Scores of roadblocks were set up, but somehow the trigger-happy trio always managed to elude them.

Newspapers headlined the story. One reporter dubbed the killer of Corporal Paul the "Trigger Woman." The name stuck.

Pennsylvania state police found the abandoned Buick and traced the licence to Henry Crawford, from Wheeling, West Virginia. Inside it they found a suit of child's clothing and a woman's red scarf. Private Moore, now out of hospital, remembered that the woman who shot his colleague wore a red scarf.

As soon as Moore was capable of making the trip, he went with Captain Jacob Mauk to Wheeling to meet Henry Crawford. The old man lived in an isolated house and admitted the two officers with some apprehension after they displayed their credentials. Aware of the character and careers of his son and daughter, he must have anticipated that one day there would be a disaster.

"Irene was here yesterday with her brother and Glenn Dague, her boy friend," he said. "She left the kid with me and went off with the two men. I've no idea where they were going."

Moore stared hard at the small boy playing with his toys on the living-room floor.

"Captain," he said eventually. "That's the kid who was in the car with the woman who shot Corporal Paul."

"We'd like to borrow a photograph of your daughter,' Captain Mauk told Henry Crawford. Dutifully he produced a recent snapshot. Next day the picture was splashed over the front pages of all the local newspapers. Now that the police knew the identities of the trio they hoped to trace them quickly.

West Virginia officers kept a watch on Henry Crawford's home, believing that the Trigger Woman would creep back sooner or later to visit her son. But she didn't. Two weeks went by, and none of the officers searching for the fugitives came upon any clue as to their whereabouts.

The first police office to see the Trigger Woman was Deputy Joseph Chapman of Arizona. A few hours later he was to wish that he hadn't done so.

On January 13th, 1930, he was standing on a street corner in the town of Florence. He watched a car as it pulled up at a refreshment stand opposite him. He noticed a striking blonde at the wheel and two men sitting beside her.

Chapman recalled the story of Irene Schroeder and her two companions, teletyped out to all police units. He was certain that one of the men in the car resembled Glenn Dague. The blonde at the wheel could be Irene Schroeder. But the other man did not seem to answer to Tom Crawford's description.

Chapman decided to investigate anyway. He crossed the street and spoke to the blonde. "May I see your driving licence, ma'am?" he asked.

The woman stared back at him with undisguised hostility.

"Who the hell are you?" she demanded.

"A deputy sheriff," Chapman replied.

"Oh, that's different. Just a minute." She opened her handbag and fumbled in it. When she removed her hand it wasn't holding a driving licence – it was gripping a .38-calibre revolver. She thrust the muzzle into Chapman's chest and rapped: "I don't like deputy sheriffs. They shouldn't be allowed on the streets. Get into the car."

As she spoke her two male companions also drew guns, which they trained on Chapman. Reluctantly, the officer got into the back seat of the car. Irene Schroeder stepped on the accelerator and the car roared down the street and out of town.

The abduction hadn't gone unnoticed. There were half a dozen people on the street who saw what happened and they were quickly telling their stories to the police.

"They're headed towards Maricopa county," one man said excitedly. The sheriff phoned his buddy Sheriff Charles Wright in Chandler, Maricopa, and detailed deputies Lee Wright, Shirley Butterfield and Joseph Smith to set up a roadblock half a mile east of Chandler.

Deputy Wright was the second officer that day to look upon the attractive features of Irene Schroeder. He lived long enough to regret it, but he didn't live much longer.

The three deputies spotted the car when it was a mile from them and, as it approached, Lee Wright signalled it to stop. It bore down on the officers, weaving crazily from one side of the road to the other. Suddenly, there was a burst of gunfire. Butterfield staggered, wounded in the leg. Lee Wright's gun fell from his hand as three bullets smashed the bones of his arm.

The car slowed and the abducted officer, Deputy Joseph Chapman, was hurled out through a rear door. A bullet fired by Glenn Dague shattered Chapman's elbow as he hit the road before the car sped off into Chandler, leaving three wounded men in its wake.

Deputy Chapman, it turned out, had been right on one point. The Trigger Woman and Glenn Dague were in the car when he first spotted it, but the third occupant was not Tom Crawford. Listening to the conversation in the car when he was held prisoner, Chapman gathered that Crawford had deserted Irene's gang a week previously, in order to strike out on his own. The new recruit had been picked up along the road in New Mexico.

With two of his best deputies injured, Sheriff Charles Wright had to organise a makeshift posse. Within an hour more than 100 armed men had volunteered, and on this occasion the trail of the Trigger Woman and her accomplices proved relatively easy to follow, because their car had broken down after a journey of some 40 miles in the barren desert directly south of Phoenix.

The nearest habitation was an Indian reservation near Laveen. The three fugitives made themselves known as people willing to do some rapid business, and rented three horses from an Indian named Lone Sun Dust. They paid cash in advance, left a handsome deposit, and headed towards the Gila River.

An aeroplane accompanying the police posse soon spotted them. They had settled on a hideout in the Salt River Mountains and barricaded themselves in among the lonely granite peaks.

When the spotter plane radioed back the fugitives' position, Sheriff Wright decided on a strategy he hoped would not incur any more casualties. He split his posse into two sections. The main section advanced on the mountain hideout from the front; the second one deployed to the flank and climbed the peak from the rear.

Both groups had to do a lot of climbing. They toiled up the lonely crags, guns ready for a surprise battle. The rear section made the best time. Reaching a position a little higher than the lair where the fugitives were holed up, they let themselves down, hand over hand, to a point where they could rush the trio.

At that moment, however, Irene Schroeder spotted the front advance of the first section, now scarcely 200 yards away. The former waitress now morphed into a battle strategist.

"Shoot the dogs, sweetheart!" she shrilled. "Let 'em have it! Don't let 'em get us alive!" Before she finished her orders, a barrage of bullets echoed around the mountainside.

Rifles from the police posse in front answered in unison. Before the fugitives could fire again, another sound made them turn. They saw themselves covered by the guns of the Sheriff's second section that had come up behind them.

The battle in the mountains was over.

Waving a white handkerchief, Irene stepped forward and surrendered to Sheriff Wright. Deputies only relaxed after they had manacled the two men.

Irene's clothes were in tatters, her hands torn and bleeding from the sagebrush and mountain crags. Her shoes were reduced to ribbons of leather, her feet were scratched and blistered, and she seemed just about all in. But defiance was still written all over her face.

"Well, boys," she jeered at the posse. "Here I am, the girl you always wanted, the nation's girl friend. I'm the one you've been looking for, and here I am."

The two men with her said nothing. They didn't speak,

either, as they were returned to police headquarters in Chandler.

Irene, however, had something on her mind as she was driven back to the town. "Sheriff," she said, "I want you to do something for me." Her voice became strangely soft. "I'd like you to wire home for me. I must know how little Donnie is. I love him." She added in a low voice: "You know, he's all I've got now in the world, apart from Glenn."

A fingerprint check revealed the identity of her new recruit. He was Tom Wells, known as "Red," recently released from a New Mexico prison, where he had served a term for armed robbery. He was charged with shooting Deputies Chapman, Butterfield and Lee Wright. Irene and Glenn Dague were held to await the arrival of the Pennsylvania Police and extradition to that state.

Dague was a vastly different man from the ex-insurance salesman who had started out with high hopes of banditry. He was now very bitter towards his mistress. "She caused all this trouble," he said. "And now I'm finished with her."

He changed his mind, though, when he saw her again at the arraignment. A woman admirer of Irene in Phoenix had sent her a completely new set of clothes with which to face the judge. Dressed in her new outfit, she entered the courtroom through a gauntlet of gawping spectators.

She scowled back at them. "I ought to charge all these people fifty cents a look," she said.

Dague, who 24 hours earlier had foresworn his love, now smiled and said, "Hello, honey."

Irene flashed him a warm smile. When she saw that he was unshaven and wearing leg irons, she turned indignantly to the sheriff and demanded: "Why don't you let him shave? Why do you make him wear those awful irons? Do you think he's going to run away?"

On an impulse, she threw her arms around her lover's neck and kissed him passionately, then took a handkerchief from her pocket and carefully wiped the lipstick from his face.

Suddenly, as the charge was read out to her, she denied that she was Irene Schroeder – a fact that both she and Dague had already admitted, anyway – and now insisted that she was a respectable married woman named Mildred Winthrop.

Could this be possible, or was it a piece of desperate tomfoolery? A check was hastily put in place. On January 24th the Pennsylvania police officers who were to escort Irene and Glenn Dague back to New Castle arrived. Among them was Private Ernest Moore, now completely recovered from his injuries. He took one look at Irene Schroeder and identified her positively as the woman who had wounded him and murdered Corporal Paul.

"He's a liar!" yelled Irene. "I've never seen him before in my life. Take him away!"

The pose didn't last, however. Realising that the game was really and truly up, she not only acknowledged her identity, but began to glory in it. She regarded her journey to New Castle as a triumphal tour. Huge crowds gathered on railway platforms as her train passed through the intermediate stations. She waved to them regally and signed autographs that read, "Irene Schroeder, Trigger Woman."

As the train pulled into the station at New Castle, Glenn Dague and Irene Schroeder indulged themselves with a long, lingering kiss, vowing to love each other until the day they died. As it turned out, that day wasn't so far distant.

Shortly after they were transferred to the county jail, Deputy Lee Wright died in Arizona of a gangrene infection from his bullet wounds. Tom Wells was promptly charged with murder. He was tried within the week, found guilty and hanged.

Sheriff Charles Wright now made it known publicly that if Dague and Irene escaped with short sentences in Pennsylvania he would demand their return to Arizona to answer for Lee Wright's murder. As it turned out, his fears were unwarranted.

Irene was brought to trial during the first week in March. Up to that time no woman had ever been executed in Pennsylvania. That tradition was seriously threatened when the jury foreman read out the verdict: "Guilty of murder in the first degree, with the death penalty."

Irene listened to the verdict with no more emotion than a block of granite. Her three sisters, who attended the trial, wept copiously. Irene chided them: "Shut up, you sissies. I can take it."

Her cell was directly above that of Glenn Dague. She told him the news when she returned from the courtroom.

"I'm sorry," he said. "How do you feel?"

"I feel fine," she replied. "They can't scare me." She added, laughing, "Come on up and see me some time."

Two days later it was Glenn Dague's turn. Like his mistress, he was found guilty of first-degree murder and sentenced to death in the electric chair.

The two killers were transferred from the jail at New Castle to Rockview Penitentiary, 180 miles way. They travelled together, holding hands in the car, murmuring words of love, exchanging kisses, still held by the bonds of their passion and their crimes.

On Death Row a partition was erected at the end farthest from the death chamber to provide quarters for Irene. No woman had ever been incarcerated there before. A door in the partition led to the forward part, where Glenn Dague's cell was located. In the death chamber itself a phone was set up with a direct line to the state house in Harrisburg, in case of a last-minute reprieve by the governor.

"If I do go to the hot seat, Glenn will want to go too," Irene said as they parted. "We love each other always to the end."

The date for the executions was set for February 23rd, 1931, at 7 a.m. Although Irene was secretly hoping that justice would be tempered with mercy for a woman who was doomed to die, in her case it didn't happen. The governor's phone line remained silent.

Most people accepted that situation. Directly or indirectly, it was pointed out, Irene was already responsible for three deaths. Lee Wright and Corporal Paul were shot down by her own hand. Tom Wells was hanged shortly after he had joined forces with her. Glenn Dague would be the fourth to die because of her.

Officially Tom Crawford, who had decided to go it alone, was never found. Texas authorities, however, announced that a man answering his description was killed during a one-man bank hold-up, although the identification was not positive.

February 23rd, 1931, dawned a grey day with a leaden sky. The prisoners were awakened at 5.30. Dague refused breakfast, but Irene ate grapefruit, toast and coffee. She asked anxiously if Dague seemed worried. She was told that he was calm, and that she would precede him to the chair. This meant that she would pass the cell where her lover awaited his final summons.

The death march began at seven o'clock. Irene wore a dress of grey rayon, with white collar and cuffs. Her stockings were beige silk, one of them rolled down to the ankle so that the electrode could be fixed to her bare leg. There was a bare spot at the back of her head where her hair had been shaved for another electrode.

She was led along Death Row by a nurse dressed in white, and by two ministers, one of whom was the prison chaplain, the Rev. C. F. Lauer, and the other was the Rev. Harold Teagarden, pastor of the church where Glenn Dague had once been an active worker. The voices of the two clergymen mingled as they recited the 23rd Psalm.

The prison authorities had thoughtfully placed a screen in front of Dague's cell, so that the lovers might be spared the last painful glimpse of each other. As they neared the screen, Irene turned to the Rev. Teagarden. "Please stay with Glenn," she said. "He will need you now more than I do." The minister left the little procession to remain with Dague.

There were tears in the eyes of the nurse as they entered the death chamber, where Rockview Penitentiary's electric chair awaited its first woman occupant. But there were no tears in the eyes of Irene Schroeder. She looked straight ahead as she seated herself, unaided, in the chair. She was still very young – she had celebrated her 22nd birthday only a few days previously – but with death only a few seconds away her iron courage did not fail her. Although the prison chaplain stood close to her as the straps and the mask were adjusted, she said nothing.

The chaplain stepped back. The switch was thrown, and at 7.10 a.m. Irene Schroeder was pronounced dead.

As her body was lifted from the chair, placed on a stretcher and rolled into the post-mortem room, the sound of voices chanting a prayer was heard outside the death chamber. Glenn Dague was about to begin his last mile.

Accompanied by the chaplain and the Rev. Teagarden, he entered the death chamber and quickly sat himself in the chair. He closed his eyes as the straps and electrodes were adjusted.

A short time later the two bodies lay side by side in the post-mortem room. Glenn Dague, the devoted Christian family man who once sold insurance and who gave it all up to follow his murderous lover, had followed her once again – involuntarily, and for the last time.

truecrimelibrary

at your bookshop now, or use the coupon below